P9-DDP-031

Blairsville Junior High School
Blairsville, Pennsylvania

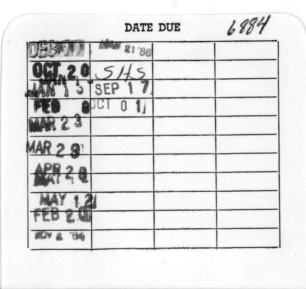

DATE DUE   6884

DEC	MAR 21 '86	
OCT. 20	SHS	
JAN 15	SEP 17	
FEB 8	OCT 01	
MAR 23		
MAR 29		
APR 28		
MAY 10		
MAY 12		
FEB 26		
NOV 2 '84		

978
L

Lauber, Patricia
        Cowboys and cattle ranching
                X38472

6884

Blairsville Junior High School
Blairsville, Pennsylvania

COWBOYS AND
CATTLE RANCHING
Yesterday and Today

COWBOYS

CATTLE

Yesterday

AND

RANCHING

and Today

BY PATRICIA LAUBER

ILLUSTRATED WITH PHOTOGRAPHS

THOMAS Y. CROWELL COMPANY · NEW YORK

6884

978
Lau

By the Author

BIG DREAMS AND SMALL ROCKETS

COWBOYS AND CATTLE RANCHING: YESTERDAY AND TODAY

Copyright © 1973 by Patricia G. Lauber
All rights reserved. Except for use in a review, the reproduction
or utilization of this work in any form or by any electronic,
mechanical, or other means, now known or hereafter invented,
including xerography, photocopying, and recording, and in any
information storage and retrieval system is forbidden without
the written permission of the publisher. Published simulta-
neously in Canada by Fitzhenry & Whiteside Limited, Toronto.

Picture credits will be found on page 143.

Picture research by Agnes Maier
Manufactured in the United States of America
ISBN 0–690–21951–2

1   2   3   4   5   6   7   8   9   10

Library of Congress Cataloging in Publication Data
Lauber, Patricia.
Cowboys and cattle ranching: yesterday and today.

SUMMARY: A history of the American cowboy and how he
changed with the coming of barbed wire, railroads, and homesteaders. Also describes modern cattle ranching.
    1. Cowboys—Juv. lit.   2. Cattle trade—The West—Juv. lit.
[1. Cowboys.   2. Cattle trade]   I. Title.
F596.L37   1973   917.8'03'2   72–187939
ISBN 0–690–21951–2

*To Roy and Becky
Becky Ann, Carl, Jon
and Grandma*

with thanks, affection, and endless admiration

ACKNOWLEDGMENTS

In the course of two long research trips to Florida and Wyoming, I was greatly helped by many kind strangers, who gave freely of their time, effort, and expert knowledge and who also supplied me with a number of valuable technical papers on cattle breeding. In particular, I should like to thank:

FLORIDA: William B. Douglass, Turner Corporation; Dr. Tony J. Cunha and Dr. A. C. Warnick, Department of Animal Science, University of Florida, Gainesville; Dr. W. G. Kirk, animal scientist at the University of Florida's Range Cattle Experiment Station, Ona; Fred Montsdeoca, agent, Brighton Reservation; and Albert Austin, manager of the Big Cypress Ranch, Immokalee.

WYOMING: Roy and Becky Chambers and their children, who shared their lives and work with me; Roy's mother and his cousin Jimmy Chambers, who talked at length with me; and David Ricks, who, like William Douglass, provided the essential contact that made the trip possible.

CONTENTS

❦ The Cowboy ❦

In the middle of the last century a wholly new kind of American came into being. He sprang from the soil of Texas—created by the land itself and by the long-legged, long-horned cattle that roamed it wild. He spent his days in the saddle, where his life was hard, often dull, sometimes dangerous, but always free. His closest companions were horses and cattle, and with them he traveled to such far places as Kansas, Wyoming, and Montana, and on into Canada. Toward the end of the 1800's he died, mostly of barbed wire, but also of railroads, homesteaders, and changing times. But by then this new kind of American, the cowboy, had seized the imagination of people all over the world.

That is why the original cowboy lives on, although he has long vanished from the American scene. He lives on in song and story. He rides with the modern cowboy, whether on horse-back or in a jeep, pickup truck, or helicopter. And he exists for all the people who, in their imaginations, have ridden the open range with him and shared his campfire.

The open range, together with its cattle, created the cowboy. On it cattle could not be handled by men on foot, as they were in the fenced pastures of the East. Handling wild cattle on unfenced land required men on horseback. And so the cowboy was born and with him a new way of life.

The land and the cattle set the terms of the cowboy's work. His duties kept him out of doors for months on end, rounding up cattle, branding them, and driving them to market. It was work that called for very special skills in the handling of animals. It was also work that called for special virtues: the courage to face danger and the strength to endure hardship and loneliness. It was work for men who prized the rough, free life of the range over the comforts of town.

Land and cattle made of the cowboy a far-reaching figure. The years after the Civil War were the time of the great cattle drives, when huge herds were trailed northward to market. They were the time when ranching spilled out of Texas, filling the treeless, grass-covered lands of the Great Plains. The spread of ranching carried the cowboy north as far as Canada.

But by then the seeds of change were already present. Railroads had pushed westward onto the Great Plains. Because they offered a way of sending cattle to market, they made possible the great cattle drives and the spread of ranching. But the same railroads carried homesteaders and other settlers westward. Competition for land grew, and the land began to be fenced. The invention of barbed wire made the fencing possible. Cheap and strong, barbed wire offered a way of building fences in a treeless land, and it put an end to the open range.

The end of the open range swiftly led to many other changes, among them ways of breeding, raising, and handling cattle. As the cowboy's duties changed, so did the cowboy himself. The original cowboy did not belong on a fenced range. "The cowboy has left the country, and the campfire has gone out," was the way he told it in song.

Today, with the coming of modern agricultural science and modern machines, ranching is still changing. And it will go on doing so, for change of some kind is always taking place.

The cowboy died of barbed wire and changing times. Yet, like ranching itself, he was the product of much earlier changes. These began when Spanish explorers arrived in the New World, bringing cattle and horses to lands where there were none. In time the Spanish horses became the Indian ponies of the Great Plains and the cow horses of the West, while the cattle became the longhorns of Texas.

🐂 Cattle to the New World 🐂

The first cattle to reach the New World arrived with Columbus. In 1493, on his second voyage, Columbus landed cattle on the island of Santo Domingo. Later explorers from Spain also brought cattle, horses, pigs, and other domestic animals to the islands of the Caribbean, where they carved out and stocked huge estates. The Spanish conquerors of Mexico did the same.

The Spanish cattle thrived in Mexico. On the central plateau they grazed a high, fairly dry land with a warm climate, much like the grasslands of Spain. They bred and steadily increased in number.

In 1540, nineteen years after the first cattle had reached Mexico, Coronado was preparing to explore lands to the north. With no difficulty, he was able to gather five hundred head of cattle for his expedition. These five hundred cows, calves, and bulls were the first cattle to cross the Rio Grande into what is now the United States. They served as a walking food supply during the vain search for treasure on the Great Plains.

5

If cattle became too lame or tired to go on, Coronado left them behind. Those that he set free north of the Rio Grande probably died out. They would have been too few and too scattered to breed. But those that he freed in Mexico did survive. On his way north, Coronado left a number of cattle in southern Sinaloa. Twenty-five years later, another Spanish explorer arrived in that province and found thousands of cattle running wild.

The grassy plateau of Mexico was a natural home for Spanish cattle. Seed, or breeding, stock of a few hundred head multiplied into thousands. By 1600 there were herds that could be counted in tens of thousands. Ships loaded with hides sailed eastward from Mexico to Spain.

To the north of Mexico there was another huge natural pasture: the Great Plains. But these vast grasslands held little interest for the Spaniards. As Coronado had discovered, there were no riches to be had on the plains—no gold or precious stones, no fabled cities. There was only the grass, stretching on and on, the buffalo that grazed it, the Indians who hunted the buffalo, and the sky.

It was not until 1690 that the Spaniards first tried ranching north of the Rio Grande. In that year some two hundred head of cattle were driven north, not onto the open plains but into eastern Texas. They were seed stock for a settlement near the Louisiana border. This settlement, like many that followed, was a mission ranch. It was run by priests for the purpose of carrying Christianity to the Indians. It was supported by the raising of cattle.

The cattle were raised chiefly for their hides and their tallow, the fat used in making candles and soap. They were tended by

(RIGHT) *California vaquero.*
(OPPOSITE) *Rodeo on a California ranch.*

mission Indians, whom the priests trained as vaqueros, or mounted herdsmen. The mission Indians, together with the vaqueros of Mexico and later of California, were the forerunners of the American cowboy.

California mission ranching began in 1769, when a ship named the *San Carlos* landed at San Diego. Aboard were colonists for the mission, several head of cattle, some hens, and supplies for starting a settlement. In the years that followed many ranches were started in California, some run by priests and some by lay settlers. By the end of the century, California had nearly a million head of cattle and was selling or bartering huge quantities of hides and tallow to traders who arrived by ship.

Emigrants to Texas attacked by Comanches.

Ranching might have gone on flourishing in California for many years except for one thing: the discovery of gold. In January, 1848, gold was discovered at Sutter's Mill near Sacramento. By 1849 the gold rush was under way. Tens of thousands of people headed for California by land and by sea.

The mobs of gold seekers who swarmed through California all had to eat, and they ate up the cattle. The demand for beef wiped out the huge herds. The same swarms of people brought an end to the big ranches and the open range. Fortune hunters who had failed to strike gold settled down to farming. The land was divided into smaller parcels, and the open range gave way to farms.

The next cattle to reach California came from Texas. Ranching there had got off to a much shakier start. Yet it was Texas that gave rise to cattle ranching in the United States.

In California, ranching had been successful from the start. In Texas, it proved nearly impossible. Texas settlers faced a problem unknown in California: the Plains Indians, chiefly the Comanches and Apaches. These were bold and warlike Indians, who posed a constant threat to the outsiders who settled their lands. Skilled and daring raiders, they struck with the speed of lightning and withdrew as fast. Their speed was due to something they had acquired from the Spaniards themselves: the horse.

When the Spaniards came to the New World, they brought large numbers of horses. The horses, like the Spanish cattle, did well. They were so much at home in the New World that they could survive, breed, and multiply in the wild, and many of them did.

(LEFT) *Comanche chief.*
(BELOW) *Vaquero.*

Wherever the Spaniards went, they took their horses and cattle with them. On long marches, some of the animals escaped, while others became lame or sick and were left behind. Where cattle and horses were being raised, some animals strayed from their ranges. Others were stampeded by Indians or herds of buffalo or lightning. As a result, big herds of horses came to live wild in the

New World. They were there for the taking by any man who could ride them.

The coming of horses made the Indians better hunters and mightier warriors. Mounted on horses, they could travel farther and faster in search of game. They could attack a more distant enemy. They could raid a settlement and escape before the enemy had recovered from his surprise. By 1700 the Plains Indians, mounted on Spanish horses, had become the terror of the more settled Indians of the Southwest. In time, they brought ruin to many of the Spanish settlements.

The mission ranch started in 1690 near the Louisiana border was the first of a number of missions and colonies in eastern Texas.

The cattle that the settlers drove north did well, but the settlements did not. By 1770 they were in serious trouble. Cattle raising was almost the only occupation in Texas. Yet there was no market for beef or hides, and it was forbidden to ship cattle to French-owned Louisiana. Even worse, the ranches, missions, and settlements were often raided by the Plains Indians. Buildings were burned, cattle slaughtered or run off, and horses captured.

Although some managed to hold on, many ranches and settlements had to be abandoned. Meanwhile the cattle thrived. They thrived on ranches and they thrived in the wild. And so the stage was set for what happened next.

In 1821 the first English-speaking colonists arrived in Texas. Soon the colonists met the ranching industry of the open range. They met herd-owning Mexican ranchers. They met the mounted herdsmen, the vaqueros. They met huge numbers of cattle, some with owners and some without. It was this meeting, this coming together of cattle, men, and horses on unfenced land, that produced the Texas cowboy.

(OPPOSITE) *Round-up on a Kansas ranch in the 1890's.*

↻ The First Cowboys ↻

In 1821 Stephen F. Austin led a colony of English-speaking Americans from Missouri into Texas. At the time, Texas was a province of Mexico, which had just won independence from Spain.

Like the Spanish settlers before him, Austin did not try to settle the grasslands of western Texas. The grasslands were high, fairly dry land with no woods and little water. They were also the home of Plains Indians. Austin chose instead to settle in eastern Texas, along the Brazos and Colorado rivers. Here the land was wooded, well watered, and fertile. Here the colonists would feel at home, since the land was much like that they had left behind. Here, also, the Indians were generally peaceful.

From the beginning, however, there was always some trouble with the Indians. Before long there was also trouble with the Mexican government. So many families from the United States were moving into Texas that the Mexican government became alarmed. It passed strict laws to control the Texas area. The

12

English-speaking settlers rebelled, and fighting broke out. In 1836 they declared Texas an independent republic.

In December, 1845, Texas joined the Union. This event angered the Mexican government, which still claimed Texas, and war broke out. It ended in 1848 with victory for the United States.

Between 1821 and 1848 there had been little peace in Texas. The English-speaking Texans had warred with the Indians and warred with Mexican troops, both of whom fought from horseback, attacking suddenly and withdrawing swiftly. In order to survive, the Texans soon learned to fight by the same methods. Many of the men who went to Texas knew how to ride, but the fighting put them on horseback and kept them there. It taught them to ride with the skill and daring of the Mexicans and Indians.

Their riding skill served the Texans well in war. It served them equally well in cow hunting, which started as a sport but later became something very different.

The English-speaking settlers had found cattle almost everywhere they went in eastern Texas. The animals—once tame, all descended from Spanish cattle—had learned to live like wild things. In the brush country of southeastern Texas, they lived in little bunches, taking cover in the thickets by day and coming out to graze at night. The cattle were as alert as deer and fiercer than the buffalo. Their great horns could gore and kill a horse or man.

The early settlers thought of the cattle as game animals, as something to be hunted along with deer and antelope. To them cow hunting was a dangerous and exciting sport and also a way of getting food.

The revolution in 1836, however, had drawn thousands of American volunteers to Texas. Once the Mexican army had been pushed south of the Rio Grande, groups of these young men began to drift toward the Mexican ranches that lay between the Nueces River to the north and the Rio Grande to the south. Here the land was well watered and, in the mild climate, grass grew green much of the year. Here huge herds of cattle were thriving on Mexican ranches.

The young men who were drifting south of the Nueces called themselves cow hunters. But they were not out for sport. They planned instead to raid the ranches for their cattle.

Some of the Mexican ranchers had fled. Others, who had fought on the Texas side, had stayed. To the cow hunters it made no difference, for in their eyes no Mexican had any rights. There were cattle to be had, with and without owners. The cow hunt-

Oklahoma cowboys of the 1880's.

ers meant to take them, and they did. They raided the range and drove the cattle north in herds of several hundred head.

This activity soon brought the hunters a new name: cowboys. The name was an old term that dated from the American Revolution. Then certain Tory snipers were known as cowboys because they hid in bushes and jingled cowbells to lure their enemy within rifle range. Now, starting in the late 1830's, "cowboys" began to mean men who rounded up and herded cattle from horseback.

The cowboys worked in groups, rounding up cattle on the river plains or beating thorned thickets to flush them out. The cattle were herded into pens and held until they numbered several hundred. Then ten or fifteen cowboys would head the herd north at a hard run that settled in a walk or trot after the first day. Within two or three days the cattle could be handled almost as easily as tame stock. The cowboys drove them on to the well-watered pastures of eastern Texas. Many Texans had received large grants of land and were looking for cattle to graze their grass. The cowboys supplied them.

The cattle bred and multiplied. By the early 1840's, Texas ranchers were looking for markets where their cattle could be sold for beef.

New Orleans, now that it belonged to the United States, was one such market, and starting in 1842 Texas cowboys regularly trail-drove cattle there. Four years later the first big northern drive on record took place. One thousand head of Texas cattle were driven to Ohio, fed and fattened, and sold.

In the years that followed, more and more Texas cattle went north along the same trail that Texas-bound settlers had followed south. It was a trail that led through Indian country. When the cowboys left those dangers behind, they immediately met new

1874 cartoon portrays "experts" hunting ticks.

ones: armed farmers and cattle raisers of Kansas and Missouri, who feared the cattle ticks that dropped off Texas herds. The Texas cattle were immune to the disease carried by the ticks, but the cattle of Kansas and Missouri were not. Their owners were prepared to shoot to keep Texas fever out of their herds.

Still, the Texans continued to trail their cattle north, first to St. Louis and later to other Missouri towns—Kansas City, Westport, and Independence. These towns offered excellent markets. Here local dealers bought and fattened Texas cattle for shipment east. Here, too, westbound pioneers were fitting out their wagons, and army quartermasters and Indian agents were buying beef. In 1854 some fifty thousand Texas cattle crossed the Red River, on the way to northern markets.

By then the drives to California were also under way. The routes were long and hard, for they led through the lands of hostile Indians, across deserts, and over mountains. But in the beef-hungry California of the gold rush, cattle sold for five to ten times what they had cost in Texas. The California drives lasted only a few years, but Texans learned from them that herds could be driven far to market, against great odds and with great profit.

Apart from that, the early drives did not count for much. They did not develop a dependable market for Texas beef, and they hardly touched the growing supply of cattle. By 1860 Texas had between three and a half and five million head of cattle.

Before the Texans could discover what to do with all these cattle, the Civil War began. Most able-bodied men went off to fight for the Confederacy. For four years there was no one to ride the far ranges and work the cattle. Herds scattered and wandered into the brush. The cattle continued to thrive, for they possessed a remarkable ability to survive in the wild. Calves were born and grew into cows and bulls that had never seen a rider or felt a rope.

When the men of Texas came home at the war's end, their state had one thing to offer them: cattle. By the summer of 1865 millions of cattle, many of them unbranded and unmarked, were roaming the unfenced ranges of Texas.

By this time, however, a great change was taking place in the United States. The North was rapidly becoming industrialized. Factories attracted hordes of workers from the farms and from abroad, turning villages into towns and towns into cities. The cities could not feed themselves.

After the war, the Texans set about moving their cattle toward the meat-hungry cities of the North. The movement gave rise to the great cattle drives and created both the cattle kingdom and its cowboys.

Front Street, Dodge City,
Kansas, in the 1870's.

✪ The Long Drives ✪

The big cattle drives of the West took place in the twenty or so years following the Civil War. Cattlemen have estimated that during this time some ten million cattle were trailed out of Texas to markets and ranges in the North. About thirty-five thousand men, a third of them Mexicans and Negroes, took part in the drives. With them went one million horses.

The cattle in this huge flow of men and animals were Texas longhorns. For the most part, they were descended from several kinds of cattle brought to the New World by the Spaniards. Over the years they had adapted to their new home, becoming taller, longer legged, and broader horned, and developing the instincts needed for survival.

It was their long, twisted horns that gave the Texas cattle the name "longhorns." The horns, which went on growing until an animal was twelve or fifteen years old, sometimes reached tremendous size. There are records of steers whose long, curved horns had a spread of nearly eight feet. But those were giants. The average spread was more likely to be four or five feet.

If the horns were long, so were the tails and legs—some tails were so long that they dragged on the ground. The legs, which ended in steely hoofs, were not only long but sinewy. With these legs the longhorns could run like antelope, climb the highest mountains, and cross the roughest ground.

In body the longhorn was tall, bony, and long backed, with flat sides and narrow hips. In color he could be anything—black, any shade of brown or yellow, blue, mouse colored, or slate. Some coats were solid colors. Others were brindles. There were coats of one color splotched, speckled, or peppered with another.

Longhorns were slow growers, as cattle go. They were not considered mature until they were four or more years old. Steers did not reach their full weight of one thousand to sixteen hundred pounds until they were eight or ten. But they grew like oaks, sturdy and strong.

Longhorns being driven through the streets of Dodge City.

The longhorns were suited to the open range, where they had learned to live without the help of man. They were also suited to the long drives north. Without the long legs and hardiness of the longhorns, it is doubtful if the Texans could ever have trailed their cattle twelve hundred to fifteen hundred miles to market. And that is what they set about doing at the war's end.

In 1865 cattle could be bought in Texas for three to four dollars a head. The same cattle could be sold in northern markets for ten times as much—if a way could be found to get them there. The only possible way was to walk the cattle to market. The Texans began gathering up herds and driving them north.

By 1866 several railroads had crossed the Mississippi and

Texas longhorns being loaded at Abilene, Kansas.

They could live almost anywhere. In Texas they were at home on the coastal prairies, in the timbered areas, in the hot, dry brush country, and on the higher lands of the north and west. The same stock was at home in the swamps of Louisiana. And before the century was out, longhorns had adapted to the cold and snowy winters of Wyoming, Montana, the Dakotas, and Canada.

They could endure heat, hunger, and thirst as well as the cold. They could find food in drought or snow. They could smell water four to ten miles away. Longhorns would attack and drive off packs of wolves. They had almost no herd diseases. And they could continue to breed nearly twice as long as modern cattle.

neared the edge of the Great Plains. The aim of the Texans was to drive their cattle to railheads, the farthest points the rails reached, in Missouri and eastern Kansas, where the cattle could be sold and shipped east.

In the first year of the drives, some 250,000 cattle were trail-driven north out of Texas. Their destination was Sedalia, Missouri, the railhead of the Missouri Pacific. From there cattle could be shipped to St. Louis and other cities. But the trail was uncertain and uncharted, and disaster lurked at every turn along the way.

On the first part of the drive the Texans found themselves trailing half-wild cattle through timbered, hilly country, where streams ran deep between steep banks. To the north they met armed mobs. Some were farmers who feared the spread of Texas fever among their own stock. Others were cattle thieves, ready

Kansas Pacific trains leaving Abilene for the markets at Kansas City.

to stampede the cattle and even murder the cowboys in order to steal herds. The worst of the cattle thieves infested the roads of southwestern Missouri that led to Sedalia.

The Texans were forced to seek other routes. Some turned eastward, heading their cattle along the Missouri-Arkansas line, and heading for St. Louis or some town east of Sedalia. But the wooded, hilly country did not lend itself to cattle drives. Others turned west, following the southern boundary of Kansas until they were well out on the grassy plains and away from settlements. They cut north through Kansas, then turned east to St. Joseph, Missouri, where cattle could be shipped to Chicago.

The problems of 1866 were great, and the Texans did not make much money from their cattle. But the drives taught them that the cattle trails of the future would have to lie to the west. The open grassy plains might be inhabited by warlike Indians, but they were much to be preferred to the timbered land and armed mobs found to the east.

The next year, however, things took a turn for the better. The first cow town of the West was established at Abilene, Kansas. The idea of a cow town had been thought of by a young livestock dealer from Illinois, who saw the need for a fairly safe place where Texas cattle trails running north would meet a railroad that was advancing west. At this place sellers and buyers could meet, and the railroad would carry the cattle eastward.

In 1867 Abilene was little more than a huddle of log huts, most of them roofed with dirt. But this was to the good. In Abilene there were no armed and angry mobs. Also, the country around it was unsettled and offered plenty of water and excellent grazing. This meant that if the market for cattle was poor, there

Abilene, looking north from the Kansas Pacific tracks.

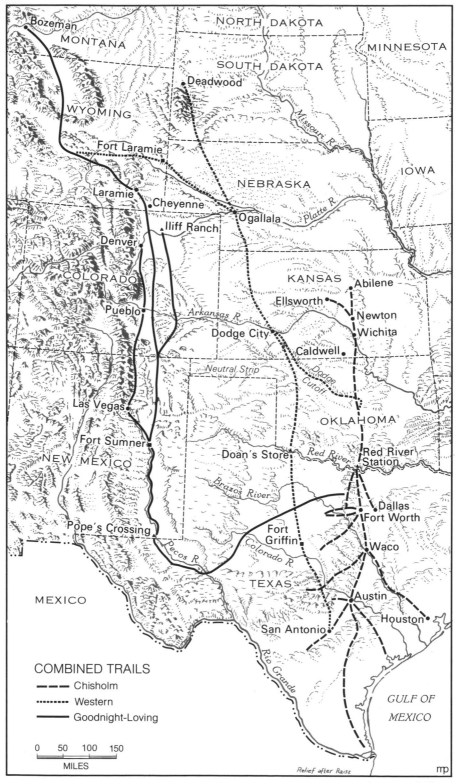

NORTH DAKOTA

MINNESOTA

Bozeman

MONTANA

SOUTH DAKOTA

Deadwood

WYOMING

Missouri R.

Fort Laramie

NEBRASKA

IOWA

Laramie

Cheyenne

Ogallala

Platte R.

Iliff Ranch

Denver

COLORADO

KANSAS

Abilene

Ellsworth

Newton

Pueblo

Arkansas R.

Dodge City

Wichita

Caldwell

Neutral Strip

Dodge Cutoff

Las Vegas

OKLAHOMA

Fort Sumner

NEW MEXICO

Doan's Store

Red River

Red River Station

Brazos River

Dallas
Fort Worth

Pope's Crossing

Fort Griffin

Colorado R.

Waco

Pecos R.

TEXAS

Austin

MEXICO

Houston

San Antonio

Rio Grande

GULF OF MEXICO

COMBINED TRAILS

- - - Chisholm

······ Western

——— Goodnight-Loving

0   50   100   150

MILES

Relief after Raisz

mp

(OPPOSITE) *Kansas City stockyards.*

was no need to sell them. They could be held on the range until prices improved. Or, if a herd was worn thin by a long, hard drive, it could be held outside Abilene and fattened up before being sold. To become a cow town, Abilene needed only stockyards, cattle pens, and loading chutes. These were soon built.

It was late in the season when Abilene opened for business. Even so, some 35,000 head of cattle passed through it on their way to Chicago and cities farther east. Two years later some 150,000 longhorns were passing through the stockyards and loading chutes of Abilene.

The main route to the town was the Chisholm Trail. On a map it looks like a frayed rope, because of all the smaller trails feeding into it from the ranges of eastern and central Texas. Over the

years hundreds of thousands of cattle followed the Chisholm Trail north, their hoofs cutting a broad river of brown in the green grass. It was a trail that offered good grazing, level land, and streams that were easy to ford. Yet it also offered the Chickasaw Indians, who levied a grazing tax of as much as fifty cents a head on all cattle passing through their lands. And before long there were also farmers armed with guns to keep the Texas fever off their land.

Gradually, the drives began to swing farther west. At the same time, railroads were advancing onto the Great Plains. New cow towns sprang up where cattle trails and railroads crossed. The most famous of them all was Dodge City, Kansas, remembered even today as the most colorful, lawless, brawling cow town of the West. Here, as in the other cow towns, cowboys with money in their pockets cut loose after months on the trail. But here, too, were the markets. Here buyers and sellers met. Here the railroads carried away the longhorns of the Texas range. Here was the trail end of the famous long, long drives.

♫ On the Trail ♫

The long drives that ended at cow towns and railheads had their beginnings in Texas at spring roundup time, so that the trail herds could start north at a time when the grass was coming on fresh and green.

At roundup time the cattle owner would cut out, or separate from the herd, animals that were ready for market or for northern ranges. Often two or more owners threw their cattle together into one big trail herd. In the late 1860's, one thousand head of cattle were counted a good-sized herd. As Texans gained experience on the trail, the herds grew in size, coming to number twenty-five hundred to thirty-five hundred head.

A trail boss, or captain, was hired to take charge of the herd, men, and equipment. He chose from among the cowboys the men he wanted for the drive, taking one man for every 175 head of cattle. Only the best of the cowboys went on the trail, for the hours were long and the work was hard and often dangerous.

Each cowboy setting out on a drive took eight to ten horses with him.

The herd of horses, called the *remuda*, was taken care of by the wrangler, who was the youngest of the trail hands. His job was to see that the horses were watered and grazed and kept from straying, and to have them gathered into a band whenever the cowboys might want to change mounts. The wrangler had to know every horse by sight and name and be able to tell at a glance if one was missing.

The wrangler usually trailed with the chuck wagon and was expected to haul wood and do other chores for the cook.

(ABOVE) *Wrangler ropes a horse from the remuda.*
(OPPOSITE) *An outfit gets ready to move.*

The chuck wagon carried everything that was likely to be needed on the trail—bedrolls, food, supplies, medicines, pots and pans, tin dishes, buckets, water barrels, the toolbox, and spare wood. Pulled by four horses, the wagon was driven by the cook. He was usually an older man than the cowboys, and he was second in rank to the trail boss. The cook was a key man because he prepared all the food that anyone ate during the long months on the trail. A good cook who made strong coffee and light biscuits could do a lot to keep the men happy and satisfied. In addition, the cook served as doctor for the men and horses, and some cooks were willing to pull teeth and cut hair.

The trail boss and cowboys with perhaps three thousand long-

(ABOVE) *Dinner at the chuck wagon.*
(TOP) *The cook inspects the stew.*
(OPPOSITE) *The drive goes on.*

horns, the wrangler with 120 horses, the cook with his chuck wagon—that was the outfit that set out in the early spring on a trip north that would take from two to four months. For the first few days the cowboys pressed the cattle hard, covering twenty to twenty-five miles a day. The cattle were as wild as buffaloes and difficult to handle. The cowboys forced the pace in order to trail-break the herd, to hurry it away from the home range, and to tire the cattle so that they would lie down at night.

By the end of the first few days the herd had organized itself into a traveling unit. There was always a natural leader, usually a steer, who took his place at the head of the herd and kept it day after day. Behind him, strung out in a line that might be as much as two miles long, came the rest of the herd, winding across the plains like a many-colored ribbon. The stronger, rangier cattle were in the lead, with the weak or lazy ones bringing up the rear.

The men, like the cattle, had their places. The most able and experienced cowboys rode point, the position at the head of the herd. Their job was to keep the herd on course, to avoid mix-ups with other herds on the trail, and if the cattle were startled, to try to keep stampedes from starting. Other cowboys, known as swing riders and flank riders, traveled beside the cattle. At the end were the dragmen, or drag riders, whose days were spent "eating dust" and urging the stragglers along.

Cowboys sifting a herd through a range count before trailing them to the railhead.

The trail boss saw to everything. He circled the herd. He rode ahead to lay out the trail if it was new, to find water, and to choose campsites and bedding grounds for the cattle.

With the home range left well behind, the trail boss planned to cover ten to fifteen miles a day. By the time the first light streaked the sky, the cook had the fire going and breakfast ready and was shouting, "Roll out! Come an' get it!" The men ate quickly, saddled up, and got the herd strung out and grazing. They let it graze for two or three miles before starting to drive it steadily along. If possible, there was a stop for water around noon. The men ate, changed horses, and started the cattle moving again.

At sundown the herd was thrown off the trail to graze. Later the cowboys drove it onto the bedding ground and rode around it in slowly tightening circles. Forced in together, the herd lay down.

By then the cook had set up camp, got the fire going, and had supper on. The men ate, sitting cross-legged on the ground, and if they were not too tired, passed the time by talking, telling jokes, or singing songs of the trail. Otherwise, they rolled into their blankets and went to sleep, except for those who were riding night watch on the herd.

The watch changed at 10 P.M., midnight, and 2 A.M., but the routine was always the same. The men rode slowly around the bedded-down cattle, and most sang or hummed as they rode. The rhythms of the songs were slow, matching the steps of the night

horses, and the tunes were mournful. Some cowboys sang hymns. Some sang of their work:

Oh say little dogies when are you goin' to lay down
And quit this forever shiftin' around?
My horse is leg-weary and I'm awful tired,
But if you get away I'm sure to get fired.

The cowboys believed that their songs soothed the cattle and kept sudden noises from startling them into a stampede. But the cowboy sang for himself as well in the loneliness of his night watch on the vast and open plains.

Around midnight the cattle stirred, got to their feet, and then lay down in a different position. The night watch went on, ending with breakfast at daybreak. Horses were saddled and then the cattle were started north for another day on the trail.

Waking a night rider.

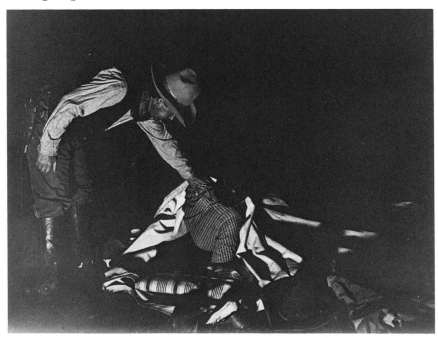

On the plains the country was flat and open, unbroken by hills and valleys, timber or brush. The only natural obstacles were the rivers. In spring, as the snows of the Rockies began to melt and the rains came, there were times when the rivers flooded beyond their banks. Usually, however, they were wide but shallow and could be crossed by wading.

The best and safest river crossings were known to the trail bosses. A good boss had his herd well strung out and walking briskly as it approached a crossing. If the lead cattle were thirsty, they would wade right in to drink. Pressed and shoved by the cattle coming behind them, the lead cattle were forced out into and across the river. The job of the cowboys was to keep the line of cattle moving across and to prevent it from bending and spreading downstream.

Crossings, however, were not always that simple. Any small thing, such as a duck taking flight from the water, might stampede the herd. The same kind of mob fear might make them balk and refuse to cross. Sunlight on the water had to be just right before the cattle would wade in. They did not like to cross with the sun in their eyes. And they might refuse to cross at all if they could not clearly see the far bank.

Lack of water was a far worse problem, though. The dry drive, across a wide stretch of land where there was no water or where it had dried up, was the most terrible experience of the trail. For all their toughness, for all their ability to endure, the longhorns needed water. They could go one day, two days, even three days without it. But by then certain disaster lay ahead. Holding the cattle at night required all hands, for they would not lie down. By day they milled about, the leaders wandering aimlessly and the rear overtaking the lead. Along the cattle trails of the plains, bleached bones spoke of the fate that had overtaken men and cattle on a dry drive.

The second most terrible experience on the trail was the stampede. Much more than other cattle, longhorns were likely to stampede, to take off in a pounding fear-driven run. The reason was that they were creatures of the wild, constantly alert to danger, hearing and smelling what no man could.

The cause of a stampede could be anything—the snapping of a twig, a stray dog, an unexpected scent carried on the evening breeze, the snort of a horse. What the cowboys feared most was a dark and stormy night. A crackle of lightning or a crash of

(ABOVE) *Herd swimming a river.*
(OPPOSITE) *Colorado roundup.*

thunder would be answered with the thud of twelve thousand hoofs. Almost before the men could move, the cattle were gone.

Longhorns often stampeded as a herd. When they did, there was a chance of getting the stampede under control. The task of the men and horses was to turn the cattle so that they moved in a circle, and thus to gain control of the herd. But sometimes the stampeding herd scattered to the four winds and whole days were lost before the men could round them up and get the herd started north again. It was the loss of time and injury to the cattle that the cowboys feared. They accepted, as part of the job, the danger to themselves in chasing panic-stricken longhorns through the dark.

Stampedes, river crossings, lack of water, Indians, cattle thieves, falling horses, accidents to the chuck wagon—these were the dangers of the trail. If they were not actually present, they still threatened. Beyond the threat of danger, there was the daily grind of work: eighteen hours a day in the saddle, night watch, the nursing of cattle, the same meals served over and over again, and in all weather the ground for a bed under the open sky. The work went on for two, three, or four months, with never a day off.

Yet in this way, some ten million longhorns were trailed out of Texas. Some were sold at market. Others were used to stock the ranges of the plains as the cattle kingdom spilled out of Texas and filled a great natural pastureland that had been left untouched by pioneers, who thought of it as a barrier and a desert.

⌘ The Cattle Kingdom ⌘

In the heart of the United States, reaching from western Texas to Canada, is the vast grassland known as the Great Plains. The plains are dry. Little rain falls and there are few springs and streams. The plains are also windy. What water there is tends to evaporate quickly.

Under such conditions forests cannot grow but grass can. Grass grows where conditions are too hard for trees, but not so hard as to make all plant life impossible. And so the plains are grassland, a huge inland sea of grass, stretching on to the horizon and far beyond.

Before the coming of the white man, life on the plains was in easy balance. Land and water supported the great sea of grass. The grass supported large numbers of plant-eating animals, among them buffalo, or bison, pronghorns, rabbits, hares, and prairie dogs. They, in turn, were food for wolves and coyotes, and they were food, shelter, and clothing to the Plains Indians.

43

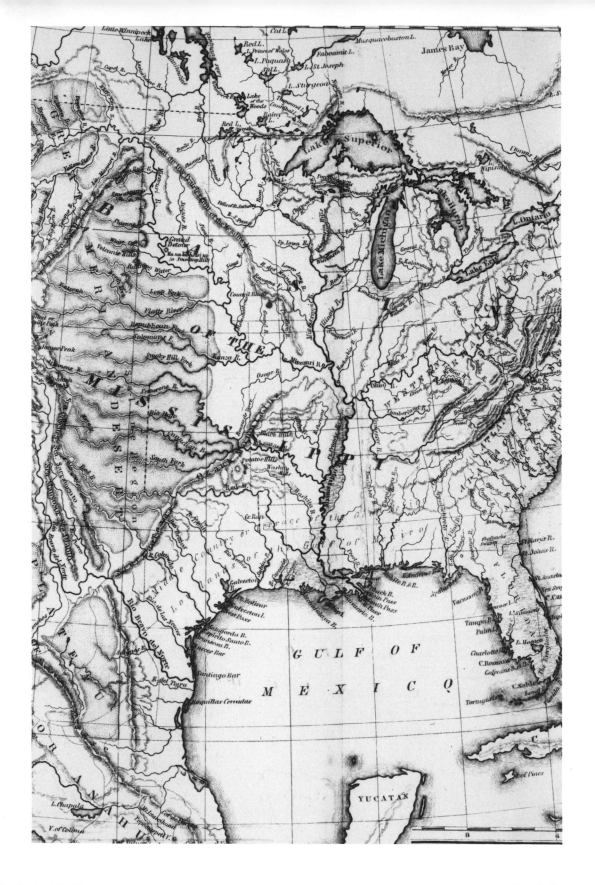

The coming of the Spaniards to the New World added another grazing animal—the horse—to the plains, but it did not change the pattern of life.

To Spanish eyes, the plains looked very much like parts of Spain, land that the Spaniards knew as good for grazing. To the American explorers and pioneers who later came upon them, the plains looked very different.

Explorers pushing westward from forested, well-watered lands crossed the Mississippi and came into a kind of land that they had never known before. The forests stopped. Ahead lay only grass—first the tall grasses of the prairies and then the short grasses of the higher, drier plains. Most explorers took this dry and treeless land for a desert, and that was how it appeared in atlases and geography books as late as 1860. Maps of the United States showed a long, broad blank space between the Missouri River and the Rocky Mountains. Lettered on it were the words "The Great American Desert—Unexplored."

Pioneers saw the plains in the same way. For several generations Americans had moved westward, felling trees, clearing land, building cabins and rail fences, and digging wells or taking water from springs and streams. The plains, however, were a land without forests, without logs for cabins or rails for fences. They were a land where water was scarce. And they were a land of fierce warlike Indians mounted on horses. To pioneers the plains were not a place to settle. They were an obstacle to be crossed on the way to the Rockies or the Pacific Coast.

Many inventions had to be made before pioneer farmers could work this land. It was not until the end of the 1800's that farmers began to move onto the plains.

Meanwhile, white hunters with long-range rifles were wiping out the great herds of buffalo that had roamed the plains. By

(OPPOSITE) *Map of the Mississippi Basin, from a school atlas of 1843. Note "Great American Desert" at left.*

(LEFT) *Apache chief
Geronimo.*
(BELOW) *Herd being driven
across a river.*

1876 the buffalo were nearly gone and so were the Plains Indians, who had been either killed or put on reservations.

The plains might have lain empty until the coming of the farmers except for one thing. This was the time of the great cattle drives. In the brief span of fifteen years—from 1865 to 1880—cattle ranching spread all over the Great Plains.

The northbound trails were rivers of longhorns, the route along which Texas cattle moved from the breeding ground of the South toward the meat-hungry cities of the North. The same flow of cattle spilled over onto the plains.

Longhorns by the thousands flowed into New Mexico, Arizona, Nevada, and Utah. They were in Colorado and Idaho, Kansas and Nebraska. They spread north into the Dakotas, Wyoming, Montana, and Canada after the accidental discovery that cattle could survive northern winters by feeding on grass that had dried on the stem in summer without spoiling and so kept its food value as hay. In just a few years cattle took up the land left empty by the buffalo, and with them went ranching as a way of life.

In choosing a ranch site on the plains, the cattleman was chiefly concerned with grass and water. He needed a place that

had both. Usually he set up his headquarters, which later became the ranch house, along a stream. Some ranchers settled on only one side of a stream. Others occupied both sides.

At first the rancher had no neighbors. His cattle roamed and grazed where they pleased. The rancher considered that the land they grazed was his range.

As time passed, other cattlemen arrived. They established themselves either upstream or downstream from the first rancher. Some miles away there was another stream and here, too, ranchers set up their headquarters. After a while the first rancher was surrounded by neighbors. They were some miles away from him, but the range—the open, unfenced land—was divided.

The ranchers had no legal right to the land their herds were grazing. The range was public land, belonging to the states or to the federal government. A rancher with tens of thousands of head of cattle might own no land at all—not one square foot of the range and perhaps not even the land on which the ranch buildings stood. But he did possess what his neighbors recognized as range rights. In their eyes he had a right to use the water of the stream. He had a right to use the land drained by the part of the stream he held.

In the earliest days of the open range, ranches were separated by unused grasslands and the stock of one ranch did not mingle with the cattle of another. Later, as the range began to fill up, ranches bordered on one another. Cattle with one brand drifted onto neighboring ranches and got mixed with cattle bearing a different brand.

Cowboys sometimes herded strayed cattle back toward their own ranges. But the chief way of dealing with these cattle was the cooperative roundup. Neighboring ranchers began to work together at roundup time, so each had help in gathering his own cattle into one herd. Roundups took place twice a year.

The spring roundup got under way with the coming of warm weather, when the tips of new grass showed green through the gray-brown of the old. This was the more important roundup, for this was the time when most of the calves were branded. If there was to be a long trail drive, cattle that were ready for market were cut out of the herd.

In the autumn roundup, calves born in late spring or early summer were branded, as were strays that had been missed in spring. If cattle were being shipped to market on a nearby railroad, that herd was thrown together in the autumn, when the animals were fat from summer grazing.

Each year the ranchers from a large district met in early spring. They made plans for the roundup, chose a roundup boss, and decided where and when the work would begin.

Two or three days before the roundup was to start, outfits from the various ranches began to gather at the meeting place. In a large district there might be two hundred to three hundred cowboys, each with ten horses, as well as fifteen or more chuck wagons and cooks. The ranch foremen met with the roundup boss to make detailed plans and to assign the men their duties. They

Early ranch in New Mexico.

Arizona Rangers.

planned with care because the job ahead was big. The roundup
might last seven or eight weeks, while the men searched for cattle
over perhaps four thousand square miles of range.

The first day's work, like that of the days to follow, started
early. By 3 A.M. the cooks were up, fires going, and coffee starting to boil. Cries of "Roll out!" and "Come a-runnin'!" mixed with
the banging of iron spoons on iron pans and brought the cowboys
to their feet. Beds were rolled and tied and breakfast quickly
eaten. By then the wranglers had brought the horses in at a run
and the cowboys chose the ones they wanted and saddled up. In
small groups they fanned out to comb the countryside for cattle
and to bring in "everything with hair and horns."

By ones, by bunches, the cattle were rounded up and headed
toward the roundup ground. Noon saw several thousand head
gathered into one herd, milling about in a cloud of dust, the air
torn by the bawling of cows and calves that had been separated

Cutting out a calf.

from each other. The cowboys turned in their horses for fresh ones, grabbed a hasty meal, and went back to work.

From the time the first herd was assembled, there were several kinds of work to be done. Some cowboys went on combing the range for cattle. Some held the herd or herds. Some set about "cutting" the herd—separating it into smaller herds, each containing only the cattle of one owner.

The rancher on whose range the work was being done had his cattle cut out first. For this work, the cowboys rode their cutting horses, which were the most agile and highly trained. Twisting and turning, the cowboys and their cutting horses worked out of the herd all the cattle bearing the rancher's brand. The calves, of course, were not yet branded, but they followed their mothers, which were.

When one cowboy cut a cow and her calf from the herd, another roped the calf and dragged it to the fire where the branding irons were heated. Wrestled to the ground, the calf was held by two men. A third drew the red-hot branding iron from the fire and pressed it quickly and carefully to the calf's side. The calf bawled. Other calves bawled. Cows bawled.

The third man quickly earmarked the calf, using a sharp knife to cut each ear in the owner's pattern. Since brands sometimes grew faint or were changed by rustlers, earmarking provided a second way for ranchers to identify their cattle.

Most of the bull calves were castrated, or neutered, at branding time to change them to steers. Steers were easier to handle and better for beef. Only the best calves were kept as bulls for breeding.

The branding, earmarking, and castrating of a calf took only a minute or two. Then the men started on the next one. All after-

Calf on its way to be branded.

*Neutering (foreground)
and branding
(background).*

noon the work went on, hot and heavy, with the churned-up dust rising in clouds and mixing with the smoke from the fire and the odors of sweat and burning hair. Finally, along about sundown, a roper signaled that the last calf had been cut from the herd. The time had come for the men to strip the saddles from their horses, wash up, eat, and then bed down for the night. Only the night watch kept up its rounds, until the cooks' cries woke the sleepers and another day began.

When the work was finished on the first range, the owner held his herd while the other cattle were driven to the next range. There the job began again, as cowboys fanned out to comb the second range for cattle. The herds grew. Calves were branded and earmarked. The night watch was ridden, and the days started so early that cowboys complained that they didn't need bedrolls, just a lantern to see by for catching a fresh horse.

From the beginning, there were as many herds as there were owners. As these herds moved from range to range, they grew bigger because cattle kept being added to them. As a result, the men's hours grew longer and their work harder. Most of them worked twelve to fifteen hours a day, and there were times when they worked eighteen to twenty hours. Still, there was a job to be done, and they did it.

On the last day of the roundup, the branded herds were started off toward their own ranges. By then nearly every animal that had drifted off its own range during the winter and early spring had been found and returned to its owner. The new calves were branded. And if there was to be a trail drive, the beef herd had been thrown together. As the spring roundup ended, the drive began.

The roundup, like the very handling of cattle from horseback, grew out of the open range. When the cattle kingdom spilled out of Texas across the plains, methods of ranching hardly changed, for the plains, like Texas, were unfenced land. Yet, even as the cattle kingdom grew, change was on the way. It was brought about by many things, but the main ones were railroads, homesteaders, and barbed wire.

Chicago Union Stockyards, 1866. (Courtesy Chicago Historical Society)

❧ Railroads, Homesteaders, and Barbed Wire ❧

Until the middle 1800's the United States was a country of small farms and small industries that supplied food and goods for people who lived nearby. In the second half of that century many far-reaching changes took place. Immigrants poured into the country. Cities grew thick with people. As the Industrial Revolution took hold, big factories sprang up, their smokestacks staining the sky as clanking, throbbing machinery turned out mass-produced goods. Railroads, which had slowly advanced across the Mississippi and onto the Great Plains, now linked east and west. They carried factory goods to faraway towns, and food from one part of the country to another.

These changes had made possible the rise and spread of the cattle kingdom. The growing populations of the industrial cities and towns offered a market for beef. The railroads, advancing westward, provided a way of reaching it. The beef market improved as meat-packing plants were established in Chicago, St. Louis, Kansas City, and other central cities. Now it was no longer

Ceremony as railroad tracks were joined to link East and West at Promontory, Utah, May 10, 1869.

necessary to ship live cattle all the way to the large cities; they need be shipped only as far as the meat-packing plants. The demand for beef grew still more as people learned to eat canned meat. It grew again with the invention of refrigeration, which meant that fresh beef could be shipped from the packing plants all across the United States and even across the Atlantic to Europe.

The growing demand for beef produced a great boom in cattle

ranching. On the Great Plains, grass and water were free. All a man needed to become a rancher was some cattle and enough know-how to handle them. Cattle could be raised with little expense and, in the good years, with great profit. Tales of the easy money to be made spread through the United States and many other countries as well. As a result, easterners and foreigners alike rushed to the plains to become ranchers.

As the range began to fill up, many problems arose. There were rustlers. There were grass pirates, men who moved onto the range and put their own brand on any unmarked cattle they could rope. There were range wars, when large numbers of armed men warred over range rights and cattle markets.

Still other problems concerned beef prices and weather. Sometimes these two kinds of problems occurred at the same time.

For example, in the late 1860's prices paid for cattle rose every year. Prices were particularly good in 1870, and so the summer of 1871 saw the greatest northbound drives in history. Some seven hundred thousand head of Texas longhorns were driven to Kansas alone. Other western states were also driving cattle to market to take advantage of the high prices.

But by that summer of 1871 market conditions had changed,

"A Dispute over a Brand."

An early herd of Herefords.

because business had fallen off in other parts of the country. There were few buyers, and half the cattle from Texas went unsold. They were held on the ranges outside the cow towns. When summer changed to autumn, the grass around the cow towns had nearly been grazed out.

Winter came early to the plains. Before autumn ended, snow was falling. All winter, blizzard after blizzard swept the plains. Icy winds howled across the land, dropping their burden of snow and piling it into drifts. Some cattle managed to work through the snow to what little grass lay beneath it. Many more failed. When spring finally came, 75 percent of the cattle left to winter over in Kansas were dead.

Many ranchers had suffered terrible losses, but even so the disaster of 1871 soon faded into memory. Cattle prices were up again. The market for beef continued to grow. And railroads continued to lay tracks across the plains, making it easier and easier to ship cattle to market.

Yet the same railroads were carrying more and more settlers west.

To encourage the builders of railroads, Congress had granted them huge tracts of land paralleling their routes. Most of this land was in the undeveloped West. Owners of the railroads were laying out towns on their land and doing all they could to get settlers onto it.

To encourage the settlement of undeveloped areas, Congress had passed the Homestead Act. It granted land, free of charge, to any United States citizen who would settle on it and farm it for five years.

The Homestead Act was passed in 1862. Millions of acres were homesteaded in the next few years, but few of them were on the Great Plains. The frontier pushed westward into the tall-grass prairies. It stopped short of the higher, drier plains, which, in any case, were still the land of the Indians and the buffalo.

As the Indians and the buffalo vanished, cattle ranchers were moving onto the plains. Soon other settlers appeared, too. They came in unending railroad carloads, and they came to farm, to homestead or to settle the lands held by the railroads. They were aided by a number of new inventions: by new kinds of farm machinery for sowing, cultivating, fertilizing, reaping, and bind-

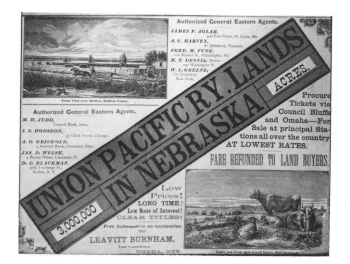

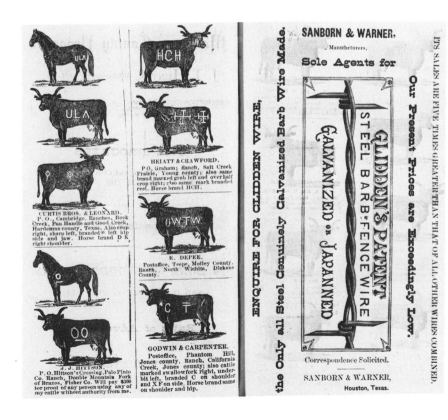

(ABOVE) *Nebraska homesteader's sod house.*
(LEFT) *Brands and barbed wire.*

ing, all of it suited to the open, level lands of the prairies and plains. The railroads brought in the goods that farmers needed and carried away their crops of grain.

The Homestead Act and the railroads encouraged farmers to go west. New machinery brought huge areas under cultivation. But it was still another invention that made it possible for farmers to settle the prairies and plains. This was barbed wire.

In 1874 the first piece of barbed wire was sold in the United States. During the years that followed, factories turned out and sold untold quantities of it. Cheap and readily available, barbed wire offered a way of fencing a land where there were no trees to fell for split-rail fences. It gave farmers a foothold in a land that was occupied by cattle. Barbed wire made a strong fence armed with barbs, or prickers, that discouraged cattle from pushing against it and breaking it. Barbed wire drew farmers, and sheep ranchers as well, onto the grassy plains of the cattle kingdom.

By the early 1880's the more farsighted cattlemen could see that the days of free grass and open range were nearing an end. The range was public land. Among themselves the cattlemen had worked out a system of range rights, but they did not own the land their cattle grazed. Range rights would not protect them against the homesteaders, who were staking out claims and fencing their land.

The wiser cattlemen began to acquire and fence all the land they could. They homesteaded along stream banks, so that they controlled the water; some had their cowboys do the same. They bought land. They leased it. What they could not homestead, buy, or lease they often fenced anyway.

The start of fencing brought on widespread fence cutting and violence among different groups. There were wars between cattlemen who fenced their land and cattlemen who clung to the idea of free grass and an open range. There were wars between

Blairsville Junior High School
Blairsville, Pennsylvania

Homesteaders cutting cattleman's fence.

cattlemen and sheep ranchers. There were wars between cattlemen and homesteaders.

In time the fence wars ended. New laws concerning land and water rights were written to fit the conditions of the plains. Then there was less cause for conflict. Even before that, several things were clear.

One was that cattlemen were going to have to share the range with the homesteaders and sheep ranchers and with others who would come after them.

A second was that barbed wire and fencing had come to stay. One day soon, there would be no more open range. Every man's land would be fenced.

A third was that ranchers could no longer leave their cattle to fend for themselves the year round. This was a bitter lesson learned in the years 1884–87.

The falling prices, shortage of grass, and blizzards of 1871 had taught no one a lesson. Prices recovered. The demand for beef kept rising. And there was a great demand for range stock, because newcomers needed cattle for their ranches. In one three-year period the price of range stock rose from seven or eight dollars a head to thirty-five. Still the boom continued as people rushed in to buy herds and become ranchers. The problems of 1871 were forgotten.

Then disaster struck again, only this time it was much worse.

By 1884 the ranges of the Great Plains were seriously overstocked. With the land forced to carry too many cattle, the once-thick carpet of grass had been grazed down to a danger point. In places where four or five acres of land had been enough to support a cow and her calf, it now took ten acres.

That year the prices paid for beef cattle began to drop, and they went on dropping for three years.

In the same period, the weather was causing a series of natural catastrophes. The plains were caught in a drought. Texas was hardest hit, but the drought affected most of the western range, where grass was already being overgrazed.

The winter of 1884–85 arrived. In late December a terrible blizzard struck. In southwestern Kansas and nearby areas, cattle turned their tails to the howling Arctic gales and began to drift south before the winds. They could not get at the grass, which lay under a solid layer of sleet and ice. The open plains offered no shelter. And so the cattle drifted on and on into what is now Oklahoma. There they met a 170-mile-long fence that cattlemen had built to keep cattle from drifting. The long strings of cattle piled up against the fence, and many froze to death. The rest got past the fence, either breaking through it or clambering over the piled-up bodies, which served as ramps. Miles to the south, at a second drift fence, the same thing happened again.

That spring cowboys found cattle from northern ranges five hundred miles south in Texas. Tens of thousands of frozen bodies were thawing out along the drift fences. Cowboys from many ranches gathered in Texas that spring to hold gigantic roundups of the surviving cattle and drive them back to northern ranges. But the drought in Texas had burned the grass and dried up the

streams. With little to eat or drink, still more cattle died. Of the thousands of cattle that had drifted south, perhaps half died that winter and spring.

Worse was to follow.

The searing dryness of the drought spread north from Texas. In Kansas and Nebraska, in Wyoming and Montana, the range was already damaged by overgrazing and the winter-kill of ice. Now it was beset by drought. To thin out the herds, to salvage what they could, ranchers rushed huge numbers of cattle to market. Market prices had been dropping. The great flood of cattle sent them tumbling. The ranchers had to sell their stock for almost nothing.

The drought continued into the summer of 1886. Springs and water holes went dry. Prairie fires swept the dry grasslands. In autumn the old hands in Montana and Wyoming noticed wild animals moving south earlier than usual. Elk began to drift away. Birds disappeared. Soon snow fell.

At first the snow was welcome, for it was taken as a sign that the drought was ending. But the early snow melted a little and then froze into ice. The cattle could not get through the ice to the grass below. In December two blizzards struck. In January another began. Icy winds howled out of the north, the temperature dropped below zero, and the snow fell . . . and fell . . . and fell. For ten days the blizzard went on. Cattle died as if they were flies. There was nothing for them to eat except the bark of trees and the tips of sagebrush that sometimes showed through the snow. They gathered around ranch houses, bawling for help and crowding up to look in windows. There was no way anyone could help them.

Spring roundup showed how bad it had been. Many ranchers had lost 90 percent of their stock. Creeks were choked with dead cattle and the skies were black with buzzards. For years afterward, the bleached bones of cattle lay scattered across the plains and the foothills of the Rockies. And in many places the once-great carpet of grass had become a stemless mass of roots.

Many ranchers decided to take their losses and quit. Others hung on and made new starts. But it was clear to them that things would never again be the same. The old ways would have to change.

Totting up their losses, the ranchers came to realize that cattle should be fed and cared for to get them through the winter. Taking care of them and buying winter feed was going to be expensive. The money would be wasted on the leggy, lean-flanked longhorns. It might much better be spent on cattle with short legs and heavy bodies, which would produce more beef and better beef.

By the end of the century, ranching was a very different industry. The open range was gone. The district roundups were gone. The long trail drives had ended. These changes foretold the end of the longhorn, of the long-legged hardy cattle that had walked a thousand or more miles to market. They foretold also the end of the original cowboy, of the men who had set their course by the Pole Star and trailed the longhorns across a world that seemed as vast as the sky above.

Barbed wire put an end to the open range.

❧ Changing Ways ❧

Longhorns were the cattle of the open range. The open range shaped them out of Spanish stock, and it made them hardy and vigorous and healthy, as able to live without the help of man as any creature of the wild. It gave them the long legs and stamina that later carried them to market. It gave them the adaptability to live almost anywhere. The cattle kingdom that occupied and ruled the plains was built on longhorns. It arose from the cheap, sturdy cattle that could take care of themselves as they roamed the open range, grazing the free grass and drinking the free water.

Then the time came when the grass and the water were no longer free, when barbed-wire fences put an end to the open range. A man who wished to become a rancher had to buy or lease land. He had to pay to fence it. Where winters were likely to be hard, he needed to put up hay and buy winter feed. Ranching was becoming expensive.

Perfect for the open range, longhorns were the wrong cattle for fenced lands that cost money.

Longhorns grew slowly. They took four or more years to mature, eight or ten to reach their full weight. Ranchers now needed cattle that matured faster, that more quickly converted grass and feed into beef.

Longhorns were long boned and lean flanked. Ranchers needed cattle with a chunkier build, cattle that carried more beef and better grades of beef.

If ranchers were going to feed and care for their cattle, they needed animals that could produce more and better beef in a shorter time. What they needed was the stocky-bodied, short-legged British beef cattle.

Some British cattle had already been brought into the northern ranges, but they were not widely raised. They were less hardy, less able to take care of themselves, and much more expensive. Also, their short legs were not suited to long trail drives.

Now, however, the long trail drives were over. The trails were rapidly being plowed under or fenced over, and, in any case, they were no longer needed. They had been replaced by railroad feeder lines, running north and south to meet the main east-west lines.

While the range was open, there had been no point in bringing in expensive bulls or cows to build up the herds. The cattle were free to roam as they pleased, and there was no way to control the breeding. Barbed-wire fencing made such control possible. Pure-bred cattle could be kept separate from range stock. Bulls could be kept away from cows except at the time of year when the rancher wanted them to breed, thus controlling the season when calves would be born. Each bull could be used to service whatever cows the rancher chose.

With fenced pastures it was possible to raise purebred herds. Bulls from these herds could be used to service cows from the range cattle. In this way, generation after generation, the range stock could be improved and built up—in fact, by such cross-breeding the longhorns were eventually bred out of existence.

Fenced pastures also enabled the rancher to control grazing and to make better use of the grass. Cattle were allowed to graze one pasture for a while and then moved to another before the first could be overgrazed.

There was no way to make all these pastures front on the streams. To provide water, ranchers had to drill wells and dig ponds. They erected windmills to catch the winds of the plains and power the pumps for the wells.

As ranching methods changed, so did the cowboy's duties. He now had to dig post holes, string and mend fences, cut and pitch

Today's beef cattle are valuable.

They are confined in pastures fenced with barbed wire.

hay, and grease windmills. His way of life also changed, for he had become ranch-based. During much of the year he slept in a bunkhouse and ate in the ranch kitchen or in the bunkhouse.

The original cowboy, the cowboy of the cattle kingdom, had lived outdoors most of the year. His duties sent him riding endlessly over the range, looking for cattle to round up and brand or trailing herds to market. His food, plain but filling, was cooked over a campfire. He slept at night with the sky as his roof.

His closest companion was his horse, but at roundup time or on a drive he had the company of other men exactly like himself. All had proved their skill at riding horses and handling cattle. All were self-reliant, because a cowboy often worked by himself or with one partner and on the open range there was no place to turn for help. Like the longhorns they herded, cowboys had to fend for themselves. They had to be men of proved courage, for

one man who failed to do his duty could endanger all the rest. Many of the cowboys were young. They were strong and healthy and full of high spirits. Together they formed a kind of brotherhood with strong bonds of loyalty.

Even if he did not go on a trail drive after spring roundup, the cowboy still spent the summer riding the range and tending cattle far from the lights of town. In some regions, herds were driven to summer pastures up the mountains, where the grass was fresh, the air cooler, and water more plentiful. If cattle were left on the same range all year round, then they had to be shifted about in summer from places where streams or water holes were drying up to where conditions were better. In addition, the cowboy looked for calves that had lost their mothers and needed to be taken care of. He looked for cattle that needed doctoring.

When summer ended, the autumn roundup began. After that, work slacked off. Many of the cowboys were laid off and spent the winter trapping or working in town. A few of the old hands were kept on to man the line camps. These camps were cabins near the edge of the outfit's range, and the men spent their days riding out to check on the cattle. They turned back stock that were drifting off the range, kept the streams and water holes open, and drove in cattle that seemed to need special feed or shelter.

By early spring, cattle were bogging down in mud. The range riders hauled them out. They noted which parts of the range the herds were grazing, information that was useful in planning the spring roundup that marked the start of the new year's work.

Living as he did, the cowboy had few possessions.

His clothing was mostly what he was wearing—a heavy cotton flannel shirt, sturdy dark-blue denim trousers that were stuffed into boots with heels high enough to keep a man's foot from run-

Oct 13 1912
Great Falls Mont

Friend Guy I received your postal and letter an was glad to here from you

You were so bussy when I left I did not get to thank you for the good time we had at the Stampede

I came west 31 years ago at that time baring the Indians an a fiew scaterd whi the country belonged to God

but now the real estate man an mister have got moste of it grass side down an most

of the cows that are left feed on shuger beet pulp

but thank God I was here first an in my time Io seen som roping an riding but never before have I seen so much of it bunched as I did at Calgary

I've seen som good wild west shows but I wouldent call what you pulled off a show, it was the real thing an a whole lot of it

those horses judging from the way they unloded them twisters wasent broke for grand mas pheaton, they were shure snakey.

an your cattil dident act like diary stock to me I dont think any I saw had been handled by milk maids

Letter to a friend, C. M. Russell. (Courtesy Amon Carter Museum, Fort Worth, Texas)

ning through a stirrup, a hat, and a bandanna. The hat was wide brimmed to keep the sun off his face on bright days and to shed rain on wet ones. The same hat was useful for dipping water, fanning a fire, or whipping an angry cow in the face. The bandanna usually served to keep the sun off his neck, but tied over his face it filtered dust out of the air he was breathing. It was also useful for blindfolding a calf or tying its feet. On occasion, the bandanna served as a towel, a bandage, or a handkerchief.

The cowboy traveled light. He carried no change of clothing, except for socks and a shirt. Besides his clothing, he owned the tools of his trade—a saddle and blanket, a bridle, a lasso, spurs, and chaps. He owned a bedroll of quilts and blankets with a heavy canvas cover. And he had a "warbag," a sack in which he kept his clean socks and shirt, his slicker, his razor, and whatever small personal possessions he had—a book, a mouth organ, a letter, or a photograph.

In the days of the cattle kingdom and before, the cowboy's life was simple, rough, and free. He lived with nature, enjoying the good and pitting his strength and skills against the bad. He summed up his life in this song:

> All day long in the saddle I ride
> Not even a dog, boys, to trot by my side.
> My fire I kindle with chips gathered round
> My coffee I boil without being ground.
> I wash in a pool and wipe on a sack.
> I carry my wardrobe all on my back.
> For want of an oven I cook bread in a pot
> And sleep on the ground for want of a cot.
> My ceiling's the sky and my carpet's the grass,
> My music's the lowing of herds as they pass. . . .

With the coming of barbed wire, that way of life passed into history. The cowboy of the future would not live under the open sky but under a roof. He would need many of the same skills, for the business of cattle ranching is raising cattle, but he would need new skills and knowledge as well.

Ranching was changing, and it goes on changing to this day.

The modern cowboy's first duty is still the care of cattle. He is expected to keep a close check on the stock. He makes sure each calf is being "mothered up." He must be able to recognize and treat the most common ailments. At branding time, he ropes, brands, earmarks, and castrates. During the hunting season he may ride from first light into the night, guarding the land and cattle against hunters and fire.

Depending on the size and kind of ranch, the cowboy is expected to be able to do a wide variety of other chores. He may spend part of the year improving pasture by irrigating it, burning brush, reseeding the land, or building dams. As well as knowing how to ride a horse, the cowboy must be able to drive a jeep and a pickup truck and to run and repair all kinds of farm machinery,

Haying is part of the modern cowboy's work.

for his duties are likely to include planting and harvesting grain and hay. He mixes feed, rides fence, puts out salt, checks water courses, and watches for poisonous plants. He helps build sheds, corrals, and loading chutes. He may even milk a few cows and clean the barns.

The modern rancher, or cattleman, has also changed. His cattle are valuable and his land is expensive. He must make the best use of both, and so he interests himself in everything from what kind of beef housewives most want to new ways of preventing disease. He turns to science for advice on feeding and breeding cattle. He uses machines, both big and small, whenever possible to do the work of men.

The chief reason the rancher does so is that cowboys are in short supply. A cowboy's life is still the dream of many young

(OPPOSITE) *Machine fills troughs on farm where cattle are being fattened for market.*

men, but few want the job with its hard work, long hours, low pay, and small chance for advancement. To fill the gap, ranchers must buy machines that can replace men. They buy machines that enable their wives and children to do jobs that used to take a man's strength. And they are glad to hire part-time help from the students, factory workers, tradesmen, and businessmen who, in vacations, live their dreams by signing on as cowhands.

(ABOVE) *Rounded up from pasture, cattle are driven toward the pens and corral.*
(BELOW) *Outside leaves of "cabbage" from which Albert has removed the hearts.*

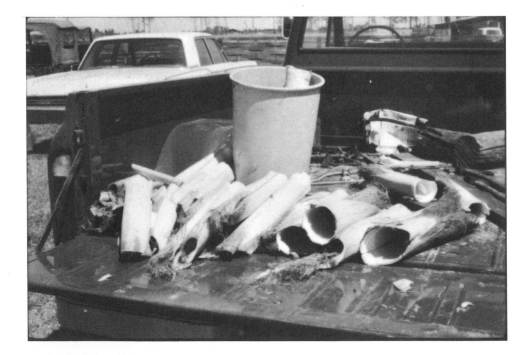

ℒ Roundup at Big Cypress ℒ

It is six o'clock in the morning. The grass is still white with the night's frost, and a light fog is rising from the ground. To the east, the sun is a dull yellow ball at the gray horizon.

The Big Cypress Ranch, however, has been astir for an hour or more. It is branding time, and a long day's work lies ahead. The early morning hours will be pleasantly cool, as the sun burns away fog and slowly rises in the sky. But by late morning the sun will be blazing out of a bright blue sky and hard on men and animals alike.

A pickup truck pulls in beside the barn and Albert gets out. He has been off cutting cabbage palm, which is to be part of the noon meal his wife will serve—the growing bud, or "cabbage," is considered a local delicacy. Albert is manager of the ranch, which is owned by a corporation, as are a growing number of ranches today. Together with his wife and daughter, Albert lives on the ranch in a small, trim house. He is its only full-time employee.

Cattle being herded into pens.

To help with the branding, Albert has hired two friends and part-time cowboys, Jerry and Franklin. Jerry works for the state department of roads and Franklin works in a factory. Both try to arrange their vacations for a time of year when their help is needed on the ranch.

Franklin has already arrived this morning and is helping Albert unload the pickup. Within minutes Jerry drives up in a sporty car, towing his horse in a trailer. The men are now ready to saddle up and get to work.

The previous afternoon they rounded up about a hundred head of cattle and left them overnight in a fenced pasture behind the barn. The first job this morning, which the men do from horseback and with the help of several dogs, is to herd the cattle into a corral, or pen.

It is one of a number of pens, which are connected by chutes, narrow passages just wide enough for cattle to pass through in single file. There are places where the chutes fork. Here, by opening or closing gates, the men can sort the cattle into various pens, according to age, sex, breed, or whatever they want.

Albert is planning to brand calves this morning. One man keeps the herd moving out of the first pen into a chute. Another, with the help of his hat or a cattle prod, keeps the animals moving along the chute. The third sits atop a two-way gate. When he sees a calf coming, he opens one gate and closes the other. When he sees a cow or steer, he closes the calf gate and opens the other.

Albert watches calf enter chute.

Cows are sorted into one pen (ABOVE) and calves into another.

The cutting out of calves goes fairly smoothly, but there are always problems when men are handling cattle in close quarters. Pileups occur as animals turn balky and refuse to move along or as one manages to turn around and tries to head back. A cow tries to lie down and gets a hoof wedged in the board siding; it takes ten minutes to free her. Every now and then, a determined cow makes a dash for it and succeeds in following her calf through the calf gate.

At last the sorting is done. The calves are in one pen. The adult animals, except for a few that got in with the calves, are in another. Now the din is tremendous, as calves bawl for their mothers and cows bellow for their young.

In the branding corral a wood fire is burning. Many ranches today use a gas fire instead for heating the branding irons, but wood fires are still common. There are a number of irons, since each calf is to be branded BC, for Big Cypress, and with a herd number.

Albert puts an iron in the fire.

Don, the accountant, records information for the herd history.

The purpose of number branding is to identify individual cattle. One part of the number tells which herd the calf belongs in and the other part is the calf's own number within the herd. An accountant from the corporation has come for the branding. He records each number and notes whether the calf is a bull, a steer, or a heifer (young female). He writes down its color and the year of its birth, as well as the quarter of the year in which it was born. Later, when the cows and calves are put back together again, each calf will seek out its mother. The record can then be completed by matching the numbers of each cow and her calf.

The herd numbers of purebred cattle are also tattooed inside the ear. In addition, some ranchers brand herd numbers on the horns, where they are easy to read.

The herd numbers help a rancher keep track of his cattle. They tell how many he has and they enable him to develop a breeding record. For example, he can tell which cows regularly produce calves, the grade of calves they have, and whether they take good care of their young. That way he knows which cows he wants to keep for breeding and which ones should be culled from the herd and sold for beef.

The rancher's records also tell him which bull he used to service each group of cows. He can then judge which bulls he wants to keep and use by the number and quality of the calves.

In modern cattle ranching, the keeping of such records is extremely important. The size and quality of the calf crop is what counts. The rancher cannot afford to keep cows and bulls that do not produce well. He cannot afford to keep cows that are not good mothers.

Big Cypress is a new ranch, and its owners are trying to build a good breeding herd. The numbers that Don, the accountant, writes down will form part of the herd history that the owners need.

By the time Albert is ready to start branding, the last member of the day's team has arrived. This is Doc, the veterinarian. He will vaccinate the calves against three cattle diseases—brucellosis, black leg, and malignant edema—and tattoo the date of vaccination in each calf's ear. He will also lend a hand with the branding, earmarking, and castrating.

At Big Cypress the earmark for a steer is a straight crop of the left ear and for a heifer an uppersquare. Like the BC brand, these particular marks are used only by Big Cypress in this county and neighboring ones. Like the brand, they identify Big Cypress cattle. They are also useful for sorting cattle as they come along a chute. The man atop the sorting gates can tell at a glance whether he has a steer or a heifer coming toward him.

(RIGHT) *Doc's table of equipment.*
(BELOW LEFT) *Vaccinating and tattooing.*

(BELOW RIGHT) *Calf's neck is clamped in squeeze chute.*

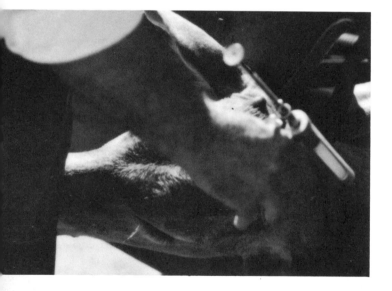

Doc has set up a table with his equipment in the branding corral, beside the calf squeeze chute. The squeeze chute does the work of the cowboys who used to throw and hold each calf that was to be branded. It is a V-shaped metal trough in which the calf is clamped against one side, which tilts to form a branding table.

Now the calves are being moved along out of a small pen into a wooden chute that leads to the branding corral. The first calf, seeing an opening ahead, plunges toward it and into the squeeze chute. One cowboy immediately shuts a metal door behind the calf, closing one end of the squeeze chute. As the calf sticks its head through the opening at the other end, a second man pulls down a lever, clamping the calf's neck against one side of the trough. A hook is released on the other side, and the side swings back on hinges. The side to which the calf is clamped is tilted sideways so that it forms a table.

One or two men hold the calf's back legs. The others set

Chute is tilted to form table, and brand is applied.

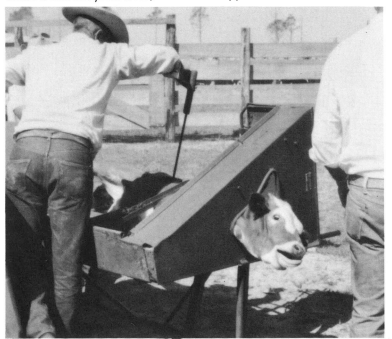

(LEFT) *Branded calf trots out of corral.*
(BELOW) *One that got away is roped, thrown, and branded in the old-fashioned way.*
 (OPPOSITE) *Calf bounds toward freedom of pasture.*

quickly to work, branding, earmarking, castrating (most of the bull calves will be neutered), vaccinating, and tattooing. The tattooing is done by Doc, who uses a kind of punch that penetrates the outer skin. He applies tattoo ink to what he has stamped in the ear.

The table is tilted back, the trough closed, and the calf's neck released. One side of the squeeze chute is swung open, and the calf goes free. It is all very quick. When everything goes well, an experienced team can do a calf a minute.

But things do not always go smoothly. There are calves that balk at entering the squeeze chute, calves that put their feet instead of their heads through the front opening, and calves that somehow manage to escape. These have to be handled in the old way. With whoops the men chase an escaped calf, grab it, and throw it. Two of them hold it, while the others set to work.

When freed, most of the calves trot or canter away through an open gate in the back of the corral. From time to time, though, one appears to think about attacking the men. It is only a calf, but even so it may weigh two hundred to three hundred pounds,

and so no one is eager to be butted by it. As they get on with their work, the men keep a watchful eye on the calf until it decides to leave the corral.

The morning wears on. The sun is high in the sky and hot. The men break from time to time to drink water from a hose, and then go back to work. Through it all, the cows and calves are bellowing and bawling. Around the branding table the air is thick with dust and smoke, and over everything hangs the smell of burning hair. Everyone is hot and dirty and glad to stop for the lunch that Albert's wife has prepared.

Albert talks a bit about his year-round work. Since this is a new ranch, one of his major jobs is improving the pasture, turning land that is not now good for grazing into land that is. Much of that land is overgrown with scrub palmetto, a small palm with stiff silvery fronds. The palmetto has a widespread root system, and so the first step is to clear the land, ridding it of palmetto roots. After that it can be harrowed, limed, and planted. It must be fertilized every year. As the amount of pasture increases and improves, the ranch can carry more cattle. In addition, Albert must string and mend fence, put out supplementary feed, repair equipment, and keep a watchful eye on the cattle. He

must treat any that are sick or injured. And he must control the breeding.

After lunch Doc takes over the discussion. He is sitting in the shade of his truck, waiting for the afternoon's work to start.

The best time for calves to be born, Doc explains, is shortly before the best grazing begins. That means the cow will get the best grass and produce the most milk at the time when the calf can best use this milk for growth.

A cow carries her calf for about nine months. So a rancher who wishes his calves to be born in a certain season must mate his cows and bulls in the season that comes nine months earlier.

During most of the year the bulls are kept separate from the cows. In the chosen breeding season, the rancher groups together the cows that he wishes to breed with a particular bull. He puts that bull in the same pasture with them. One good young bull can service twenty-five or thirty cows, provided the pasture is good. In parts of the Southwest where the grass is thin and cattle must spread out over a large area, ranchers count on one bull to every fifteen cows.

During the breeding season, there will be only a few days when a cow can conceive a calf. At these times the cow is said to be in heat. Her body has produced an ovum, or egg, and she is ready to accept a bull in mating. If the egg is fertilized by semen from the bull during this time, the cow conceives a calf. Otherwise, there is no calf.

A shout from the corral brings Doc to his feet. He lays out the equipment he needs for the afternoon's work and adds a piece of wood to the branding fire. There are other ways of branding, he says, nudging an iron into a hotter part of the fire. It is possible to brand cattle with caustic acid, but Doc thinks the acid is more painful than a hot iron. There are also experiments going on with cold, or freeze, branding. These call for dipping copper branding irons in liquid nitrogen until the irons' temperature drops to 90 degrees below zero. The extreme cold kills the pigment cells in the calf's skin. Since the pigment cells supply color, the brand comes up white.

There are two good reasons for cold branding. One is that it is painless. The other is that it doesn't scar the hide, which means that the whole hide can be used for leather. But, Doc says, white brands don't show up very well on light-colored cattle, and also it's hard to tell whether the iron has been applied long enough and the brand has taken. At present, he thinks, hot-iron branding is still the best method.

By now the men have the cattle moving through a chute toward the corral. This afternoon they are going to run the cows through—by "cows" they mean all the adults. For this they use a

Squeeze chute used for the cows.

large squeeze chute. The cow—or perhaps a bull or steer—is urged out of the wooden chute leading from a pen, into the squeeze chute. The metal door is quickly closed behind her. As she sticks her head through the opening in front, the lever is pulled and her head and neck are clamped in place. The barred sides are squeezed against the cow's flanks, for the grown cattle remain standing and must be held still.

Every animal gets a dose of worm medicine from Doc, who uses a syringe to force it down the throat. Albert looks the animal over to see if anything else needs to be done—if there is a hoof to be trimmed, horns that need cutting or sawing, a sore that should be treated. The only animals that need branding are cows or bulls that Big Cypress has recently bought.

At the end, the cow's head and neck are unclamped and the

(LEFT) *Doc sawing off horn tips.*
(BELOW) *Albert bends over to inspect teeth and mouth.*

*Released from squeeze
chute, cow heads for
pasture.*

sides of the chute loosened. The front end, which is hinged like a
door, is opened and the cow goes free. The cows generally trot
out the open gate in the corral to join the calves and find their
own. A few of the bulls and steers make a charge at the group
near the squeeze chute. Everyone is watchful but no one seems
worried. Albert is good with animals and careful about the way
they are handled. His cattle are not likely to turn wild or mean.
Usually the bull or steer veers off, runs around the corral, and
leaves through the gate. Once or twice the men wave their arms
and yell, just to make sure the animal turns away.

By late afternoon the last cow has been run through. Doc
leaves, and the other men saddle up. They herd the cattle out of
the pasture into a pen. The cattle are sprayed for flies and
mosquitoes, then driven back to a pasture away from the ranch.

The final job is to round up other cattle for the next day's work.
Albert, Jerry, and Franklin gallop off, with the dogs close behind
them. A while later they can be seen coming across the flat land.
Once the herd breaks up, but they gather it up again. A few
young animals get away. Albert and the dogs go after them.

Finally, the herd, bellowing and raising clouds of dust, pours through the fence gate into the pasture where it will be held overnight.

By this time, the light is fading and the day's heat begins to vanish. Barns and fences become silhouettes. A light breeze rustles the palm trees and stirs the leaves of the orange grove down the road. Soon the dark sky will be splendid with the stars of a clear Florida night, for Big Cypress is not a western ranch. It lies in central Florida.

In recent years cattle raising has become an important industry in the southeastern United States. Fields once planted for cotton are now pastures for beef cattle. But except in Florida, nearly all the cattle of the Southeast are raised on stock farms. Florida alone is a ranch state. It is also one that is rapidly growing in importance.

Florida today boasts some of the most modern ranches in the United States—and also the oldest roots in ranching. Among all the ranching states, Florida was the first to feel the hoofs of Spanish cattle.

⟿ Modern Feeding and Breeding ⟿

The first Spanish cattle to reach what is now the United States landed in Florida. They were six heifers and a bull that Ponce de León brought from Cuba in 1521. These first cattle were probably killed by wild animals and Indians, but before long Hernando de Soto landed more cattle in Florida, as did later explorers and settlers. Cattle were the chief source of fresh meat for the Spanish colonists and soldiers, and by the 1600's cattle ranching was a way of life in Florida.

Although it was the oldest cattle state, Florida was the last to modernize its ranching. It passed a fence law only in 1949. Until then most of the cattle in central Florida roamed an open range and lived as they had since the days of the Spanish settlers.

The fence law was passed at a time when the state's population was growing rapidly, when many industries were developing, and when both land prices and taxes were rising. Put to the trouble and expense of fencing, cattle owners were forced to take a hard look at what they were doing.

They saw that cattle raising was not worthwhile unless they did it well. Their state had plenty of water and a mild climate that allowed year-round grazing. All that was to the good. But if cattle raising was to be profitable, the ranchers needed better cattle and more cattle, and before they could build up their herds, they had to improve the pasture so that it could carry more cattle and nourish a better grade of cattle.

Improving pastures and herds is long, slow work. Even so, modern science has made it possible for Florida ranchers to take giant strides forward. Working closely with state and university scientists, they have applied modern knowledge and techniques to their lands and herds. Some of the ranch owners are large corporations with big sums of money to invest. Their ranches are among the most up-to-date and efficient in the world.

On such a ranch, pastures may be fertilized from a small airplane. Cattle are herded from one pasture to the next by a ranch hand who drives a jeep with a large "gate" attached to the front. Roads run through the ranch so that all pastures can be reached by jeep or truck. The big barns are as spick-and-span as dairy barns. The herds include show cattle that are carefully groomed each day.

The ranch manager carefully studies scientific papers on animal nutrition. Cattle, like people, need a balanced diet. To thrive, to put on weight, to bear healthy calves, they need more than just food. They need protein. They need vitamins and minerals. What food values are the pastures supplying? To find out, a rancher has his soil and grasses analyzed in a laboratory. Then he knows what he must supply through feed and mineral supplements.

In Florida several of the most common feed supplements are by-products of other industries: blackstrap molasses from the sugar mills, and citrus molasses and citrus pulp from the factories where frozen orange and grapefruit juice are canned. The supplements are placed in the pastures, where the cattle can feed on them at will. Usually they are trucked to the pastures and poured into bathtubs, since secondhand bathtubs are the cheapest large containers available.

When Florida ranchers first started to improve their herds, many of them were working with cattle known as native cows. Like the Texas longhorns, the native cows were descended mostly from Spanish cattle, with some mixture of other blood. Also, like the longhorns, the native cows had been produced by natural selection. That is, over the years they had developed into the type most fitted to survive on the open ranges of Florida. They were hardy animals that could survive poor pastures, lack of minerals, fever ticks, and hot, wet weather.

The native cows, however, were small—fully grown they weighed about 450 pounds, as compared with the 2,000-pound weight of a purebred four-year-old steer. The calf crop was also small—a cow might calve only every two or three years. Native cows were suited to surviving under unfavorable conditions, not to producing calves or beef.

Even before the fence law was passed, some ranchers had tried to improve their herds by bringing in British beef cattle. The British breeds, however, did not do well on the Florida pastures and they had no resistance to diseases such as tick fever. The ranchers then tried crossing the British cattle with the native cows. They hoped to get beefier cattle that could still do well in Florida. They also experimented with Brahmans, the humped cattle of India, which were doing well in Texas.

But real progress in breeding was impossible until several other kinds of progress had been made. One kind was bringing fever ticks and screwflies under control.

The ticks were controlled by requiring cattle to be dipped in

Brahman cow.

Santa Gertrudis bull.

a liquid that kills ticks. The screwflies were controlled in a very different way.

Screwflies are dangerous to livestock because the females lay their eggs in wounds or sores, such as those caused by branding. The eggs hatch into worms that may burrow into some vital organ and kill the animal. To solve the screwfly problem, laboratory scientists bred huge numbers of male screwflies and then exposed them to radiation. The radiation made them sterile. That is, they could still mate with female screwflies, but they could not fertilize the eggs. Planes flying over central Florida released the sterilized males at breeding time. They mated with females. Since a female screwfly mates only once during her life cycle, many of the females laid eggs that did not develop into screwworms. Repeated over several years, this program wiped out the screwfly population.

Control of diseases, fencing, better pastures, supplementary feeding—all of these made it possible to improve the herds. Today ranchers can raise almost any breed of cattle, if the pasture is good enough to support the animals.

There are now hundreds of herds of purebred cattle in Florida. There are British breeds, such as Angus, Hereford, and Shorthorn. There is the French Charolais. There are the big, humped Brahmans. And there are several fairly new breeds; the chief one is the Santa Gertrudis, which was developed into an established breed by the King Ranch of Texas, out of a cross between Brahmans and Shorthorns.

Since there is no "best" breed, ranchers choose the breeds best

A herd of Herefords.

suited to their needs. Then, by careful breeding, they try to develop good animals within their herds. They keep herd histories. They cull the herds so that they keep the best cows and get rid of the others. And they seek high-quality bulls—bulls that are proved breeders and descended from fine cattle.

Such bulls are expensive. A good bull is likely to cost several thousand dollars and a top-rank prize bull might cost ten times as much. To make the best use of good bulls, some ranches practice artificial insemination. Instead of putting the bulls out to pasture with the cows for breeding, they collect semen from the bulls about once every two weeks. The semen can be frozen and kept until it is needed. The rancher must keep track of when

Black Angus.

Charolais cow.

his cows come in heat. Then he uses the semen to inseminate the cows. In this way, he knows for sure that each cow has been serviced. He can control the calving season. And he increases the number of calves sired by a fine bull.

Florida is chiefly a cow-and-calf state. The herds are made up mostly of cows and calves because there is not yet enough good pasture to carry herds of steers and it does not pay to feed the calves until they become full-grown steers. Ranchers make more money by selling calves.

Some specialize in producing calves that are ready to be slaughtered for veal. Others sell their calves to a feeder, a man or company engaged in buying cattle, keeping them, and feeding them up before selling them for beef. The best Florida calves are shipped in double-decker trucks to feeders in the Corn Belt of the Midwest. The others are sent first to winter pastures in Oklahoma, Texas, and Kansas, and then to feedlots in California.

In choosing breeds of cattle to raise, ranchers are guided by the kind of calves they want. The man who is raising calves for veal wants cows that calve regularly, are good mothers, and are good milk producers. He wants calves that put on weight quickly and well. The man who sells his calves to a feeder is concerned with the qualities that the feeder wants. A feeder is likely to want animals that are easy to handle and that feed and flesh out alike. He wants animals that are similar in size and build. It is easier for him to sell such cattle to a meat packer.

A rancher must also decide whether he wishes to straight-breed or crossbreed. In straightbreeding the rancher works with one kind of cattle, breeding like to like: Hereford to Hereford or Angus to Angus. In crossbreeding he works with more than one breed of cattle and crosses them.

There are several reasons why he might want to crossbreed.

SIRE ROSENBERG   COW___1___

DAM 139   Date of Birth 3-15-1957 Description HEREFORD

YEAR	CALF NO.	SEX	DATE OF CALVING	SIRE	DAYS OF AGE	ACTUAL WEANING WEIGHT	ACTUAL DAILY GAIN	ADJUSTED WEANING WEIGHT	ADJUSTED DAILY GAIN	ADJ. DAILY GAIN GROUP AVE	WEA GRA
1959	209	ST	4-30	KII ZATO	180	380#	2.11	510	2.2*	2.16	2
1960	27	ST	4-16	KII ZATO	196	450	2.30	529	2.30*	2.17	?
1961	43	X ST	3-20	OLE RED	226	490	2.17	499	2.17*	2.14	?
1962	1	X HF	2-14	ROAN W.	290	560	1.93	469	2.04	2.20	2
1963	1	ST	2-22	KII	256	620	2.42	557	2.42*	2.18	
1964	1	ST	2-10	KII	262	580	2.21	508	2.21*	2.26	
1965	1	X ST	2-22	K4	258	630	2.44	561	2.44*	2.25	
1966	1	X ST	3-24	WHITES.	219	480	2.19	506	2.19*	2.26	
1967	1	X HF	2-9	WHITES.	264	590	2.23	537	2.33*	2.25	
1968	1	HF	3-13	175	229	470	2.05	496	2.15*	2.20	

A common one is to improve his herd. Suppose a rancher's stock consists mostly of native cows. To upgrade his stock, he brings in purebred Hereford bulls. The first generation of calves will be half native cow and half Hereford. He takes the heifers from these calves and, when they are old enough, breeds them with Hereford bulls. Their calves are one-quarter native cows and three-quarters Hereford. Again, he breeds the heifers and the Hereford bulls. This generation of calves is one-eighth native cow and seven-eighths Hereford. In this way, the rancher keeps building up the Hereford blood in his herd.

A second reason for crossbreeding is to try to get the best qualities of two or more breeds. For example, the French Charo-

COW _____

S OF TERING IOD	YEARLING WEIGHT	WINTER DAILY GAIN	YEARLING GRADE	120 DAY GAIN HEIFERS	160 DAY GAIN STEERS	120-160 DAY GAIN GROUP AVE	FINAL WEIGHT	DAYS ON FEED	FEEDLOT DAILY GAIN	FEEDLOT DAILY GAIN GROUP AVE	YEAR
17	570	1.29	2-		2.00	2.74	900	178	1.85	2.83	1959
LL FEEDLOT			2+		2.56*	2.35	980	206	2.57	2.29	1960
LL FEEDLOT			2-		2.37	2.71	1020	224	2.36	2.60	1961
4	720	1.19*	2+	REPLACEMENT		(CHAIN	NO. 2^2)				1962
LL FEEDLOT			2+		3.25*	2.85	1230	196	3.11	2.83	1963
54	620	74	2+		2.80*	2.66	1070	161	2.80	2.63	1964
LL FEEDLOT			2		2.69*	2.66	1160	199	2.66	2.65	1965
LL FEEDLOT			2-		2.87*	2.53	1020	202	2.67	2.45	1966
3	770	1.17	15	REPLACEMENT		(CHAIN	NO. 11^2)				1967
5	660	1.22	14							·	1968

Cattle may be sold at the ranch where they were raised or, as here, at auction.

Brahman hybrid steer.

lais are large, muscular cattle with big bones, long legs, and long bodies. Their beef is low in fat, which means that there is less waste. A rancher might decide to cross Charolais with a British breed in an effort to get the body of the British breed and the leaner meat of the Charolais. He cannot be sure that crossbreeding will give him what he wants, but he may think it is worth trying and decide to raise herds of crossbred cattle.

Some ranchers crossbreed for still another reason. They find there is extra growth in calves produced by crossing a purebred cow with a bull of a different breed. This extra growth is called hybrid vigor. (A hybrid is a cross between two different strains or breeds.) Hybrid vigor in calves means that they are stronger, healthier, and more resistant to disease. They gain weight faster. They weigh more at weaning age, when they are old enough to stop nursing, and they reach slaughtering weight at a younger age. This means that their beef is more tender. Still more important, it means that they do not have to be fed so long—that it is cheaper to raise them.

This extra growth is most likely to occur when Brahmans are crossed with a British breed. The two are not only different breeds but also different species. Also, the extra growth occurs only in the first cross. Suppose a rancher is crossing Brahman bulls with Hereford cows. Their calves will have hybrid vigor. To go on getting hybrid vigor, the rancher must keep his Brahman and Hereford stock pure. He keeps crossing them for calves and selling the calves. He does not raise and breed animals that are half Brahman and half Hereford unless he plans to cross them with still a third breed, which will again give him hybrid vigor.

Crossbreeding of any kind is much more complicated than straightbreeding. It is more difficult and more expensive. And the calves are less likely to be alike in size, shape, and other characteristics. That is why many ranchers prefer to straight-breed and to concentrate on producing good purebred animals. Others, however, have been successful at crossbreeding and believe strongly in it.

No matter which method the rancher prefers, ranching today is very different indeed from the time when cattle ran wild and only the fittest survived. Breeding, feeding, and good management are the keys to successful modern ranching. Conditions vary from one part of the United States to another and even from ranch to ranch, but the keys remain the same. They are the same on the new ranches of Florida and on the huge and famous old ranches of the Southwest. They are also the same on small family ranches, where these still exist.

In many ways the small rancher, like the small farmer, has a difficult time today. He lives in a big country with a big population, where conditions favor the mass producer of foods or goods. The owner of a big ranch deals in large sums of money. He can buy first-rate bulls. He can buy an expensive machine for haying that lets two men do the work of ten or twenty. His herds and lands are large enough to make the machine pay off.

The small rancher is more likely to straightbreed than to experiment with crossbreeding, because it is expensive to build up and maintain herds of different purebred cattle. He is more likely to buy the service of a good bull than the bull itself. He personally owns only the most necessary equipment. The rest he shares with his neighbors. They buy machinery together and take turns using it. They also work together, each helping his neighbors with branding and other big jobs. In fact, the small rancher can survive only with the help of his wife, his children, and his neighbors.

It is not an easy life, yet most small ranchers would not trade it for anything else in the world. Most of all they prize their independence, their right to make their own way and to make of themselves what they wish. But they also prize their closeness to the earth, their sense of being part of nature, as the earth revolves around the sun and the changing seasons bring changing chores.

(ABOVE) *The rich grasslands of Jackson Hole make fine grazing.*
(BELOW) *The homestead cabin that Roy's parents built now serves as the bunkhouse.*

☙ The Year at the Flying V ☙

Jackson Hole is a broad green valley, lying high between two mountain ranges. It is in northwestern Wyoming, one of the most beautiful and interesting parts of the United States. The area is famous for the hot springs and geysers of Yellowstone, for the clear streams that are born in the jagged, snow-capped mountains, and for its wildlife—bear, moose, antelope, deer, elk, and dozens of others. It attracts tens of thousands of campers, fishermen, and hikers every summer.

Much of the region has been made into national parks, forests, and monuments. But tucked in among these public lands there are still a number of ranches. The grazing in and around Jackson Hole is some of the finest in the world.

One of these ranches is the Flying V, which is owned and run by the Chambers family: Roy, his wife Becky, and their three children, Becky Ann, Carl, and Jon. They make their living by raising cattle and also by running a small dude ranch. The dude ranch lies a few miles away from the cattle ranch, up the Gros Ventre Valley.

In this part of Wyoming, winter comes early and lingers long. The heavy snows may start in December and continue into April. Winds may reach gale force—forty to forty-five miles an hour—blowing into roof-high drifts snow that was four to five feet deep on the ground. In this cold and snowy weather, the chief ranch activity, and almost the only one possible, is feeding the stock. The Flying V carries about three hundred head of stock over the winter.

The cattle are kept in a feed ground, a fenced pasture that has no irrigation ditches running through it. (When the ground is snow-covered, ditches are hidden and cattle may fall into them. A cow that gets on her back in a ditch cannot get up.) To feed them, Roy hooks up a sleigh to a team of horses or a tractor and loads it with bales of hay. With Becky or the children helping him, he drives through the feed ground. One by one, the bales are kicked off the sleigh and the cattle, following behind, start to feed. A cow eats about thirty-five pounds of hay a day.

The horses must also be fed. They are kept separate from the cattle because the two eat in different ways. A cow eats and eats and eats, cramming down all available food. Then she lies down and chews her cud "at leisure." A horse does not chew cud and it eats more slowly. When cattle and horses are together, the cattle get more than a fair share of the hay and can starve the horses to death.

Roy's other regular winter chore is milking Beulah, who is the milk cow and a Holstein. Beulah is a very motherly cow. Given a chance, she will adopt any kind of young animal—a kitten, a baby chick, or another cow's calf.

With the stock fed and Beulah milked, the Chamberses have time for winter sports, for skiing and snowmobiling, and for going to cutter races, which are competitions among small, horse-drawn sleighs. Winter is also the time for visiting friends and neighbors. Around Jackson Hole most of the year's social life is packed into the winter months. If Roy and Becky take a vacation, they usually go away in February, a time when there is so little to do on the ranch that Roy need only find someone to do the feeding and milking.

By March ranchers in other parts of the state are busy with outdoor chores, but around Jackson it is still winter. Roy is now checking and mending equipment. Becky has started spring housecleaning, for when spring really comes she will be too busy with other work. The children are in school.

In April the winter quiet ends and the new year's work begins. Around Jackson, April and early May are the time of year when calves are born, so that cows and calves can take full advantage of the short summer.

The Flying V usually has between 150 and 175 cows. Of these at least 130 will calve during a five- or six-week period. The weather in April is still bad—cold, snowy, and windy. So Roy and Becky, helped by the children, spend much of their time out of doors checking the cows. They check at dawn, at noon, and every hour or two in the afternoon, riding through the feed ground in the jeep or on the tractor or on horseback. The worse the weather is, the more often they check the cows. In very cold and windy weather, they go on checking every hour or two at night. Night is the time when there is most likely to be trouble, because more calves are born at night.

Several things can go wrong during calving. Sometimes the calf is too big for an easy birth. Sometimes it is in the wrong position. Its head may be twisted or its feet turned. Or the body may be emerging tail first, which means that the calf may start to breathe before its head is in the air. In such cases, Roy or Becky must help with the birth, gradually pulling the calf free or turning it so that the birth is normal.

Carl drives tractor pulling trailer with baled hay.

In a normal birth, the amniotic sac that has enclosed the calf breaks and the calf is born totally free of it. But in some births the sac does not come off. The cow will lick at it, but human help is sometimes necessary to get the sac off the calf's head so that the baby can breathe.

Even if the birth is completely normal, wind and cold can kill a calf that does not get up and start nursing soon enough. There is also a danger that a calf will fall sick with pneumonia or some other disease. When Roy is checking the cows, he carries medicine with him and he may treat a sick calf on the spot. But if the weather is very cold or the calf can't get up and suck its mother, he takes the sick calf back to the house.

The traditional way to warm up a cold, sick calf is to put the animal in a bathtub of warm water. It is still a good method, but the problem, Becky finds, is that she then has an eighty-pound wet calf to deal with in her small kitchen. She prefers to warm up a calf with an electric blanket and a hair dryer.

Depending on how sick and weak the calf is, Roy may treat it in the house and then put it back with its mother, or he may put cow and calf in a feed stall in the barn, or he may keep the calf in the ranch house, taking it out to suck its mother and then bringing it back.

In spite of all this care, it does sometimes happen that an animal dies. A cow may die while giving birth. Roy may then give her calf to Beulah, who has calved a month earlier and by April has milk enough for two or three calves. Or perhaps there is another cow whose calf has died. Then Roy gives her the motherless calf.

Many cows will not accept or care for a calf that does not belong to them. They know their own calves by smell and they reject a stranger. Long ago cattle owners worked out a way of persuading a cow to accept a strange calf in place of her own. They do it by skinning the dead calf and tying the skin on the calf they want to put in its place. After a few days the skin can be removed.

The same method is used if a rancher wishes to transfer a calf from one cow to another. Some cows are better mothers than others. They have more milk and they take better care of their young. If a good mother loses her calf, the rancher may give her the calf of a bad mother, a cow that does not take good care of her young or that is likely to go dry. That way the calf will be better fed and better cared for.

By the time calving ends in May, the winter's snows have melted. Some blustery days still lie ahead, but summer is fast approaching. It is time to start mending fence, planting oats as feed for the coming winter, and dragging the meadows—smoothing out the surface by breaking up gopher mounds and big clods of manure with a tractor-hauled drag machine. It is time for Becky to start opening up the dude ranch. It is time for Roy to start working with the cattle.

Roy works two herds of cattle. One is a breeding herd, which he uses to produce bulls that he sells. This herd is made up of cows, calves, and bulls. Bull calves that do not meet Roy's standards are turned into steers and thrown in with the other herd to be raised for beef.

The other herd is made up of what are called grade cattle. It consists of steers, which will be sold for beef, and of cows and their calves. There are no bulls in this herd. Roy uses bulls from his breeding herd to service the cows among the grade cattle.

The cattle in both herds are Herefords, as are the cattle on the neighboring ranches. Since the ranchers share various ranges and there is no way in range country of completely controlling mating, all the cattle must be the same breed. Hereford is the one that Roy and his neighbors have chosen. Occasionally a rancher may buy calves of another breed, but they are all steers.

By the second week in May, Roy is working the grade cattle. Before they can be turned out on the range, the calves must be branded, earmarked, and vaccinated. All the bull calves are castrated and turned into steers. At this time all the cows, steers, and year-old heifers are run through. Each animal is checked for sores or signs of disease. Hoofs are trimmed. Since these are grade cattle, horns are cut and dehorning paste is put on the nubbins. Cattle without horns are easier and safer to handle. Even more important, they take up less space in feedlots and when being shipped, and are less likely to injure one another.

Roy and Ed running a cow through.

The work is done by Roy and his neighbors. When they have finished one man's herd, they do another's. Cattle that have been branded and run through are then put out on the range nearby. The range is public land, part of a national park, and the ranchers pay a grazing fee to use it. (Much of the land in Jackson Hole has been bought up and given to the federal government so that the natural beauty of the area can be preserved. But the ranchers who had grazing rights on the land before it was added to the park have lifetime use of it.)

The weeks pass and May turns into June. The weather is fine now, with fair, warm days and cool, clear nights, and it will continue fine, with hardly any rain, until September. But with the coming of summer, the pressure of work increases. The ranchers must accomplish much of the year's work in these few months, getting their cattle out on the good green grass and at the same time preparing for the winter ahead.

In June, life at the Flying V changes. Becky moves up to the

(BELOW) *Becky making bread in the kitchen of the dude ranch.*
(OPPOSITE: LEFT) *Janet and Becky Ann have just finished cleaning a cabin.*
(RIGHT) *Grandma cuts Carl's hair.*

dude ranch, for she is in charge of running it and of the dudes. This particular summer she will be extra busy, because the cook she hired earlier has decided to get married instead of coming to work. Becky must do the cooking herself, in addition to her other jobs. For help she has Janet, a young girl from Montana who has come to Wyoming for a summer job, and Becky Ann. Janet and Becky Ann will do the cabins, wait on table, and wash dishes.

Meanwhile, Grandma, Becky's mother, has come out from Michigan to do the cooking on the cattle ranch. Grandma's three "steady customers" are Roy, Carl, and Ed—Ed is a biology student and football player from Ohio who spends his summers working on the ranch. But she also feeds Jon, the youngest of the children, who shifts back and forth between the dude ranch and the cattle ranch, and any number of other people who happen to be at the cattle ranch near mealtime.

As soon as possible in June, Roy wants to brand the calves of

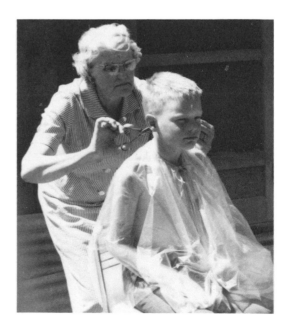

his breeding herd, run the adult cattle through, and get the herd out to pasture. With these cattle, he keeps a herd history.

Each of the April heifers is branded, vaccinated, and given a herd number, which is tattooed in the ear. As the heifers go through, a number is painted on the side of each. When the cows are run through, a different set of numbers is painted on them. Later on, when the cows and calves are back together, Roy goes through the herd and records the matches—that calf number 5 belongs to cow number 273. This information fills out his herd history.

The older heifers are run through and checked. If they are growing horns, half-pound horn weights are attached to the horns. The weights cause the horns to grow down and turn in. Such horns look better on the cattle and are also safer; the cattle

(ABOVE) *Roy attaches a horn weight.*
(RIGHT) *Herd number is easy to read on the horn.*

are less likely to get them caught in bushes or fences. By the time a heifer is three years old, her horns are long enough to brand with her herd number. A number branded on a horn is easy to read at breeding time, when a rancher needs this information for his herd history, whereas a number tattooed in the ear can be read only if the cows are rounded up and run through.

Roy looks over the bull calves. He chooses the best—those with the heaviest builds, best bones, best faces, and other characteristics that he wants—to raise as bulls. The others will be turned into steers. The steers are branded with a Flying V on the side, since they will eventually be going on the range with the grade cattle, and dehorning paste is applied to their heads. The bull calves are not dehorned and they are given only a small Flying V brand on the upper leg. Most of them will be sold to other ranchers and branded again.

Once the breeding herd has been branded and run through, it is turned out to pasture. Roy keeps checking on the herd to make sure that no calf has reacted badly to its vaccination and that no steer continues to bleed from being castrated or dehorned.

Irrigation is the other big job in June. Since most of the summer rain falls in May and September, the hayfields and pastures must be irrigated to bring on the grass.

All the water within Wyoming belongs to the state. To use water from a river, a rancher must have water rights, which are granted by the state. Once granted, the rights go with the ranch. That is, if the ranch is sold, the water rights go with it.

Each rancher with rights is entitled to a fair share of the water. Since there are no meters or gates to measure and control each man's share, the ranchers have to work things out among themselves. If one man finds he is short of water, he usually calls on those who are upstream of him to see if they are using more water than they are entitled to. Sometimes, in a dry year, there is not enough water for all. Then the ranchers with the oldest rights are entitled to go on taking water. The newcomers are cut off, starting with the last man to acquire water rights.

The main water supply for the Flying V is the Gros Ventre River, which flows into the Snake. Water is taken off the river in a canal called Savage Ditch, which is shared by various ranchers in the area. Water from the canal feeds irrigation ditches, which

Roy has dug through pastures and hayfields with a V-shaped plow. Water coming off the canal into a ditch flows through a big piece of galvanized pipe, with a metal slide at one end. The slide can be raised or lowered to control the flow of water.

Once water is flowing through a ditch, it is forced to overflow onto the land by the use of movable dams. Each dam consists of two heavy poles with a large piece of sturdy canvas bolted to them. One pole goes across the ditch. The other holds the canvas on the bottom of the ditch, where it may also be weighted down with rocks. The canvas blocks the flow of water in the ditch and forces it out onto the land.

Roy begins to irrigate around the fifth of June, starting with the land where he will later cut hay and continuing for about thirty days. Then he starts on the pastures, which he irrigates several times during the summer to keep the land wet and the grass growing.

Once irrigation starts, someone has to keep moving the dams. The dams, which are set in twos, are first placed near the control gates. In the hayfields they are moved once every hour and a half, so that the water keeps spreading over another part of the field. The first dams to be set are the biggest, heaviest, and farthest from the ranch. Moving them, which is known as "changing the water," is Ed's job. He drives a pickup truck out to the dams, hauls them out of the ditch, and places them in the next spot Roy has chosen.

When the dams become smaller and are an easy walk from the ranch house, changing the water becomes Carl's job. By the time he was ten, he was big enough and strong enough to change the water and he began learning from Roy where to place the dams so that all the land would be irrigated. Changing the water is important, but it is not very interesting work. Carl doesn't mind,

Roy and Carl moving the dams.

though, because he likes to read. Between trips he sits at the
kitchen table with an alarm clock and a book, reading until it is
time to pull on his rubber boots and go out again.

June is also the month when Roy starts getting ready to send the grade cattle up the mountain to summer pasture. The mountain pastures are part of a national forest, but some grazing is permitted on forest land. Like water rights, these grazing rights belong to the ranches, and they date from the days when homesteaders ran their cattle on the mountain pastures.

The Forest Service plots out the ranges, or pastures, that may be used. The ranges are known by the names of the creeks that drain them—Bacon Creek, Fish Creek, and Black Rock Creek are three of them. Roy's cattle graze the range drained by Ditch Creek.

Each range is used by cattle belonging to several ranchers, who plan and work together. The group with which Roy works is called the Ditch Creek Association.

Sometime in spring, ranchers of the Ditch Creek Association meet with a ranger and forester to decide how many cattle are going up the mountain and where they are to graze. The decision is based on how many cattle the range can carry without being overgrazed. It also takes into account the amount of grazing there has been by wild animals, since cattle share the ranges with elk and other grazing animals.

The ranchers, like the ranger and forester, are familiar with the land. They know where the grass is best in July and where, farther up the mountain, the cattle should be moved in August. They also know where the range is free of plants that are poisonous to cattle—lupin, which causes cows to bear deformed calves; larkspur, which kills; alfalfa, which, when it is green and growing, causes a disease called bloat and can kill.

Once the ranges are chosen and a date has been set, the ranchers hire a cowboy to go up the mountain for the summer with the cattle. Each rancher pays a share of the expenses, based on the number of cattle he will run on the range.

The cowboy's basic job is taking care of the cattle. He spends his days riding among them and checking on them. He keeps them spread out while they are grazing, so as to make the best use of the range. If they are near poisonous plants or are in places where they might fall or be hurt, he moves them. He doctors ailments. He watches out for bears and he watches out for hunters, the second greatest danger to cattle after poisonous plants.

So that the cowboy can do his job, the ranchers supply him with at least seven horses, one for each day in the week. They pay for the cow-camp supplies and provide him with a place to live, which is usually a trailer.

The cowboy comes out once a week to go into town and buy fresh supplies. Apart from his weekly trip and the times when the ranchers ride up to check on him or to help with the cattle in bad weather, the cowboy is alone from early July until late October. He is unlikely to hear a human voice, except for what comes over his radio. In his spare time, he can fish, shoot, or work on a hobby. But he must be a man who doesn't mind loneliness, as well as someone who is hardy, rugged, and healthy. He must be willing to work as long as there is work to be done with the cattle and to work in all kinds of weather, for the worse the weather is, the more restless the cattle are.

Roy says the Ditch Creek Association was lucky to find a man. Young men don't want the job, and older men are scarce. The work is hard, the wages are low, and there are no fringe benefits. Yet the job demands skill and experience, as well as a willingness to live alone—and it's one job a machine can't do.

Before the cowboy and cattle can go up the mountain, there are a great many things to be done. The trailer must be readied and supplies laid in. The cattle will need salt, and so five tons of

it are trucked up to the camp in fifty-pound blocks that the cowboy will later spread around. There are horses to be shod, for in
deep-snow country, horses do not wear shoes in winter; if they
did, big balls of snow would build up on their hoofs.

Roy works all one afternoon shoeing two horses. He trims the
edges of a hoof, smooths the bottom with a rasp, fits a shoe, and
nails it on. The nails are hammered in at an angle so that they
come out the sides of the hoof. The nail ends are cut off and
crimped. Finally Ray files or trims the edge of the hoof. It is
hard work, even for someone who is used to hard work, and a
back-breaking job. Roy is glad to finish.

The cattle have to be rounded up from the pastures near the
ranches. Roy, Carl, Ed, and two neighbors ride all one afternoon
in an unexpected snowstorm, rounding up cattle. They will make

two herds out of the cattle that are going up the mountain and put them on different parts of the range.

Not all the cattle are going up. Roy, for example, does not send his breeding herd up the mountain. If the cattle are loose, he cannot control the breeding or know which bull has serviced each cow. This year, one of the neighboring ranchers has some fine two-year-old steers, which he plans to sell in August. He decides not to send these steers up, because he feels there is too great a risk of losing some.

Among the cattle that are going up, there is some last-minute branding to be done. One neighbor has recently bought two bulls from Roy and some steers from another ranch and must put his brand on them.

Finally all is ready. Very early the next morning, as soon as there is light enough to see by, the first herd is started toward the mountain pastures. At this hour the day is cool, there are no flies or mosquitoes, and there is little traffic on the road to upset the cattle or stop their forward movement. One man rides point. The others ride beside and behind the herd.

The herd moves slowly but steadily up the mountain road. The sun is still no more than a pink glow behind the mountains. In the stillness of the day the clip-clop of hoofs, the bawling of calves, and the yips of the riders urging the cattle on can be heard a mile or more away. By five o'clock the herd is passing the dude ranch and pressing on up the mountain.

There are no serious problems, but cows keep straying off the road into the woods or turning off onto pieces of old road that are no longer used. One or more riders must go after them and get them back onto the road.

The sun is up and the air is warming when the cattle reach Horsetail Creek. Here they are turned and driven up the draw to the open pastures above and the Ditch Creek range.

That evening the men get ready for the next day's drive. Joined by Jon and a couple of other boys, the men round up the second herd of cattle and move them along the road to a bedding ground from which the drive will start as soon as it is light enough to see.

Once the cattle are up the mountain, it is nearly time to start haying. Roy is checking out machinery and discussing schedules with one of his neighbors. The two men share the swather, a big new mowing machine that does the work of three men but would be too expensive for either alone. By this time, too, the dude ranch is filling up. Becky is very busy and Roy must find time to ride with the dudes, take them rafting down the Snake River, and help in other ways. If he sees a way to take a day off, he goes fishing.

The haying looms large in everyone's mind. Once started, it will go on for ten days to two weeks, for there are three hundred acres to cut and bale. The haying starts around the twentieth of July, in the field that was first to be irrigated.

The hay is cut with the swather. Self-propelled and driven by one man, the swather has two standard mower bars, for cut-

(LEFT) *A swather.*
(BELOW) *Self-propelled baler.*

ting, and a cylinder that picks up the hay. A belt in the swather
passes the hay through a conditioner that crushes the stalks,
which are the wettest part. The hay then passes out of the
swather into a windrow, a long row, ready for drying.

Sun and wind dry the hay in about a day, and it is then ready
to be baled. There are self-propelled balers, but on the Flying V
the baler is pulled by a tractor with a power takeoff that makes
the baler work. As the tractor drives along, the baler rakes up the
windrow on a cylinder. A plunger packs the hay into a chamber,
where it forms a bale. While the hay is in the bale chamber, the
tier, or knotting machine, puts two pieces of twine around the
bale, knots the twine, and cuts it off. With the twine cut, the
baler spits out its eighty-pound bale of hay and gets to work on
the next one.

Like swathing, baling can be done by one person, driving the
tractor. Bucking bales—heaving them off the ground onto a low-
boy trailer that is pulled by a tractor or a pickup truck—calls for

(LEFT) *Tractor-powered baler.*
(BELOW) *Some ranchers collect the bales with a
forklift attached to a tractor.*

at least two strong men and preferably more. At haying time Roy hires any extra help he can find and counts himself lucky if some of Ed's friends come out from Ohio to help. In the course of a day the men will buck about a thousand eighty-pound bales off the ground onto the trailer.

Roy stacks his bales near the road, so that they are handy in bad weather. The bales are lifted onto the stack with the help of a wooden A-frame with a long boom. A rope runs through pulleys on the boom. One end of the rope is attached to a fork that lifts four bales at a time. The other end is attached to a tractor or pickup truck, which pulls the rope and swings the bales to the top of the stack. The man working there positions them in a pattern that keeps the stack firm and stable. Every rancher has his own stacking pattern. Only the bottom bales are always positioned alike. They are stacked on end so that mice cannot get at and eat the twine.

Methods of bucking bales also vary. Roy's cousin Jimmy drags

(ABOVE) *Bales are lifted onto the stack, where they are positioned by hand.*
(RIGHT) *Every rancher has his own stacking pattern.*

On the Flying V, bales are stacked with the help of an A-frame and boom.

a wagon behind his baler so that the bales land on it. Jimmy thinks it a waste of time to go back and collect the bales, but Roy thinks Jimmy's method is slow and inefficient. Other ranchers collect, carry, and stack their bales with a fork lift attached to a tractor. This method is very quick and can be done by only two men, one to drive and the other to position the bales. Roy says this is a fine way to do the job if you are stacking bales in the field where the hay was cut, but not so good if you want the stack a mile away. So he goes on bucking bales onto the trailer.

As soon as the haying gets under way, swathing, baling, bucking, and stacking can all be done at the same time—if there's enough help. Everyone pitches in. The heavy work must be done by grown men, but the children help by driving a tractor or truck. If Becky has any free time, she comes down from the dude ranch to help.

Grandma's time is spent in the kitchen. At the height of haying, she may have twelve to fourteen people to feed three or four times a day, all of them hungry and in need of hearty food. At breakfast alone, the haying crew puts away a meal of steaks, pancakes, potatoes, and eggs, washing it down with cups of strong coffee.

When the haying ends, it is time to start irrigating again, to mend fences, to take the horn weights off the breeding herd, and to work at the dude ranch, since August is its peak month. Some years Roy and his crew hire out to do custom haying at other ranches.

September is the time for threshing the ninety-day oats that were planted in early summer. When the oats have been cut and bound into small bundles of ten to twelve pounds each, the grain is shocked. Six to eight bundles are picked up and leaned together in a shock. When the shocks have dried, they are pitched into a wagon and pulled to the threshing machine. The thresher separates the grain from the stalks and blows the grain into a truck or into sacks. It blows the straw the other way. Most ranchers use the straw to add bulk to their winter feed. Some, who make haystacks instead of baling and stacking, blow the straw onto the top of the stacks to protect the hay from rain and snow.

Roy and Becky truck their oats to a granary, where the grain is stored until they need it in winter. Then they take the oats they want to a mill, where the oats are mixed with barley and molasses for a winter feed.

By the time the oats are in, summer is ending. The dude ranch is closed. Grandma has gone home and so has Ed. A touch of autumn can be seen in the trees.

September and October are fence-mending time, because as soon as the weather turns, elk will start coming down from the mountains. Most will spend the winter in a government game refuge, but there are always some around the ranch. If elk can get through a fence, they will eat the oats out of the field and any hay they can get at. In winter elk may join the cattle in the feed ground. The Chamberses enjoy watching the elk and do not begrudge them food, but they cannot afford to have elk eating up

With this tool, which takes the strain, anyone can mend fence. The job no longer requires a man's strength.

the cattle's winter food supply. Good fences are the best protection for the hay.

With the coming of September, Roy and his neighbors begin to keep a careful eye on the weather. Rain is likely and some snow may fall in the mountains. Whenever the weather looks bad, the ranchers go up the mountain to help the cowboy with the cattle. In bad weather the cattle will head for home, and one man alone can't handle them.

Before the month ends, the ranchers help the cowboy shift the cattle from Ditch Creek to Turpin Creek, which is closer to home. They also move the cow camp down the mountain, nearer the road. As autumn advances, the cowboy has more and more work. The instinct of the cattle is to drift toward home, and the cowboy must hold them on the range.

Unless there is a bad storm, the cattle stay up Turpin into October. The first to come down are the steers and heifers that are going to be sold for beef. They usually come down around the tenth of October, for by that time the mountain range is starting to dry up and they need to be put on better feed.

Roy runs his beef cattle through, checking them and doctoring them, if necessary. Then he puts them out on the pastures that were irrigated in summer. The grass is still rich and nourishing, and by now frost has killed the alfalfa. The cattle can eat it without danger of bloat.

As late in October as possible, the ranchers bring down the cattle they are not going to sell. They get the cow camp out of Turpin, and the cowboy's job is then finished.

Roy runs these cattle through. He brands any calves that were born on the range, vaccinates them, and dehorns them. The cattle usually wear down their hoofs on the range, but at this time he checks them for long feet and trims the hoofs, if necessary, so that snow will not ball up on them.

Usually there is no need to start feeding the cattle before Thanksgiving, but sometimes the snow starts early and the cattle must be put on the feed ground. If a cow has to search for food, she loses weight, and this is not good at a time when most cows are feeding one calf and carrying another.

Autumn is the time of year that Becky likes best. The summer visitors are gone from Jackson and the camping grounds. The leaves are golden. The sun is still warm, while the frost in the air tells of a winter that is not yet come. When the cattle come down the mountain, it is a kind of homecoming, a gathering in of harvest before the storms of winter.

In late October and early November the cattle buyers start to come around. Some of them work for feedlots, while others work for themselves and sell to feedlots. On his first visit a buyer is taking a look at what the ranchers have this year and sounding out the prices that other buyers are offering. Later the buyer makes an offer on the particular cattle he wants.

Jackson Hole cattle usually bring a good price because they have been raised on excellent grass and have had excellent care. If a buyer's offer is in line with what Roy thinks the cattle should

bring, he accepts it. The buyer arranges to send a truck for the cattle. His aim is to get them into the feedlot as quickly as possible and to market in January.

If Roy does not sell the cattle at the ranch, then he must find a market, a place where cattle are sold at auction. Today ranchers try to avoid shipping cattle long distances to market. There is too much shrinkage, or loss of weight, during a long trip, and the longer the trip is, the greater the risk of injuries and deaths. Roy does not want to ship his beef cattle more than five hundred miles, and so he is likely to choose a market in either Idaho or Wyoming.

After the cattle are sold at auction, they are taken to the buyer's farm or to a commercial feedlot. More and more, feedlots are local ones, because it is often better to ship the feed to the cattle than the cattle to the feed. (This trend has made Texas the No. 1 cattle-fattening state, since it was already the No. 1 cattle-raising state.) Similarly, it has proved better to send the packing plants to the cattle than to ship live cattle to the packing plants. In recent years, the meat companies have been closing down their giant slaughterhouses in central cities such as Chicago, Omaha, Kansas City, and Des Moines. They have opened smaller plants out where the cattle are.

Sometimes Becky and Roy are both able to take a few days away from the ranch and go to market. Sometimes only Roy goes. But it is always a very brief trip. As December comes on, the snow starts and the cattle must go onto the feed ground.

December is also the time for weaning the calves born in April and May. The calves start to eat grass when they are six weeks old, but now they must learn to eat hay and grain and to do without their mothers and their mothers' milk. Weaning takes about a week, with the cows in one feed ground and the calves in another and a high board fence between them. For the first two or three days the calves bawl and the cows bawl. Since there are several hundred of them, the bawling and bellowing is almost the only thing that can be heard on the ranch. Then quiet returns, and by the end of the week the calves are eating hay, although they must be kept separate from the cows for the rest of the winter.

On the ranch, life is settling down to its winter pattern of feeding the cattle and milking Beulah. Becky has long since finished putting up her jams, jellies, and fruits, and gone on to baking the cakes and cookies she will give as Christmas presents. She is catching up on correspondence, paying bills, doing accounts, and reading up on advances in veterinary medicine so that she can brief Roy on new developments.

Outside, the earth rests beneath the snow. The cows, feeding on the hay cut in summer, grow heavy with calves that will be born in April, a few weeks before the grass comes green again.

The cattle are Herefords, not longhorns, and they do not walk to market but travel in trucks. A good cowboy is hard to find, and much of the work he once did is now handled by ranchers and their families and machines. Yet something remains from earlier days that has not been killed by barbed wire and changing times. It is a way of life, a way of life shared by people who work with living things and who answer not to timeclocks and buzzers but to the changing seasons of the earth.

SELECTED
BIBLIOGRAPHY

BROWNE, EDWARD GAYLORD. *Spain in America: 1450–1580*. New York: Harper & Brothers, 1904.

*CLEAVELAND, AGNES MORLEY. *No Life for a Lady*. Boston: Houghton Mifflin, 1941.

DALE, EDWARD EVERETT. *Cow Country*. Norman: University of Oklahoma Press, 1960.

*DOBIE, J. FRANK. *The Longhorns*. Boston: Little, Brown & Co., 1941.

*———. *Up the Trail from Texas*. New York: Random House, 1955.

*———. *A Vaquero of the Brush Country*. Boston: Little, Brown & Co., 1929.

*EMRICH, DUNCAN. *The Cowboy's Own Brand Book*. New York: Thomas Y. Crowell, 1954.

GARD, WAYNE. *The Chisholm Trail*. Norman: University of Oklahoma Press, 1954.

*GARST, SHANNON. *Cowboys and Cattle Trails*. Chicago: Wheeler, 1948.

*GIPSON, FRED. *Cowhand: The Story of a Working Cowboy*. New York: Harper & Brothers, 1953.

HORGAN, PAUL. *Great River: The Rio Grande in North American History*. New York: Rinehart & Company, 1954.

*JAMES, WILL. *Cow Country*. New York: Charles Scribner's Sons, 1927.

LEA, TOM. *The King Ranch*. Boston: Little, Brown & Co., 1941.

SANDOZ, MARI. *The Cattlemen.* New York: Hastings House, 1958.

STEEDMAN, CHARLES J. *Bucking the Sagebrush.* New York: G. P. Putnam's Sons, 1904.

VANDERBILT, CORNELIUS, JR. *Ranches and Ranch Life in America.* New York: Crown Publishers, 1968.

*WARD, FAY E. *The Cowboy at Work.* New York: Hastings House, 1958.

WEBB, WALTER PRESCOTT. *The Great Plains.* Boston: Ginn and Co., 1931.

* Indicates books most accessible in style and content to young readers.

PHOTO CREDITS

The publisher thanks the following for granting permission to use photographs from their collections:

American Angus Association, 104; American Brahman Breeders Association, 102 left, 108 bottom; Brown Brothers, facing page 1, 3, 6, 14, 17, 32, 48, 49, 51, 54 top, 59, 60, 66, 68, 75 bottom; Culver Pictures, 7; Denver Public Library, Western History Department, 10, 16, 18–19, 23, 29, 52, 62 bottom, 65; Erwin E. Smith Collection, Library of Congress, 4, 33, 34 top, 34 bottom, 35, 36, 37, 38, 50, 54 bottom, 70–71, 75 middle; Florida Department of Agriculture, 105; International Harvester Company, 78; James Jerome Reference Library, St. Paul, Minnesota, 8; The Kansas State Historical Society, Topeka, 26–27; L. A. Huffmann photo courtesy of Mark Brown, 46–47, 53, 73; Patricia Lauber, all photographs appearing in Chapter 9 and Chapter 11 with the exception of page 116 and page 132 left which are by Laura Ost; Library of Congress, 24; Library, State Historical Society of Colorado, 20, 40, 41; Museum of The American Indian, Heye Foundation, 46 top; NEBRASKAland Magazine Photo, 2, 72 middle, 72 bottom, 76, 77, 98, 103, 108 top; New York Public Library, Picture Collection, 9 top, 9 below, 106–107; Walter Osborne, 72 top, C. M. Russell drawing courtesy of Montana Stockgrowers Association, 67; Santa Gertrudis Breeders International, 102 right; Solomon D. Butcher Collection, Nebraska State Historical Society, 62 top, 64; Stimson Photo Collection, Wyoming State Archives and Historical Department, 22; Union Pacific Railroad Museum Collection, 58, 61; William C. Woodbridge, *School Atlas,* 1843, Library of Congress, 44.

INDEX

ABOUT THE AUTHOR

Patricia Lauber has written numerous books for children. Some are fiction and some nonfiction, but both often concern animals, a special interest of hers. In addition to writing books, she has worked as an editor of magazines and books for young readers.

Miss Lauber was born in New York City and was graduated from Wellesley College. She has traveled widely in Europe, the West Indies, Canada, and the United States, often in search of material for her books. Research for this book took her to ranches in Florida and Wyoming, where she interviewed many people and observed everything from branding to haying at close hand. Some years earlier, she had spent a summer on a ranch in New Mexico. It was the memory of that summer, coupled with a sense of changing times and changing ways, that gave rise to the idea for this book.